Johannes Bendzulla

White Cube, White Teeth

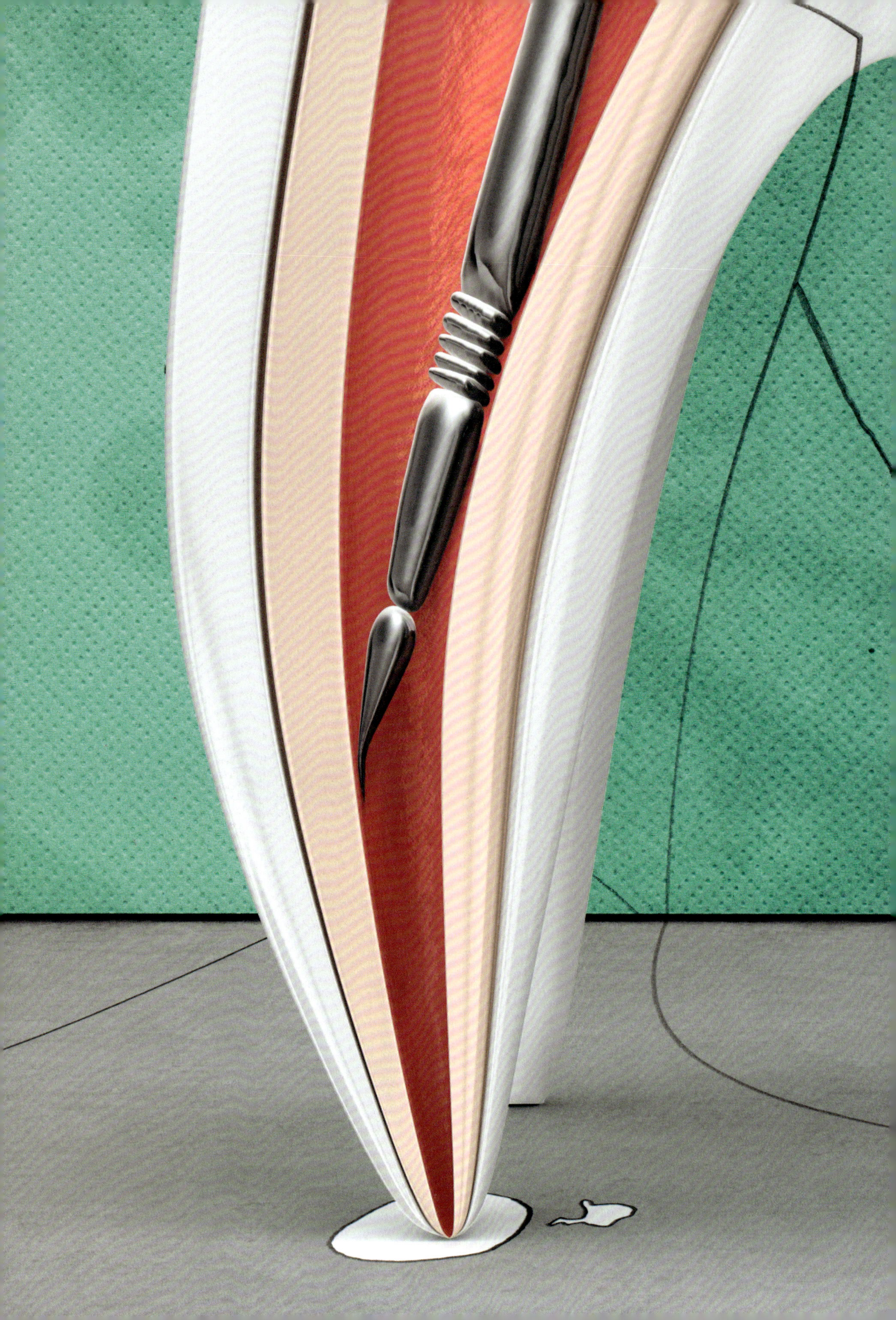

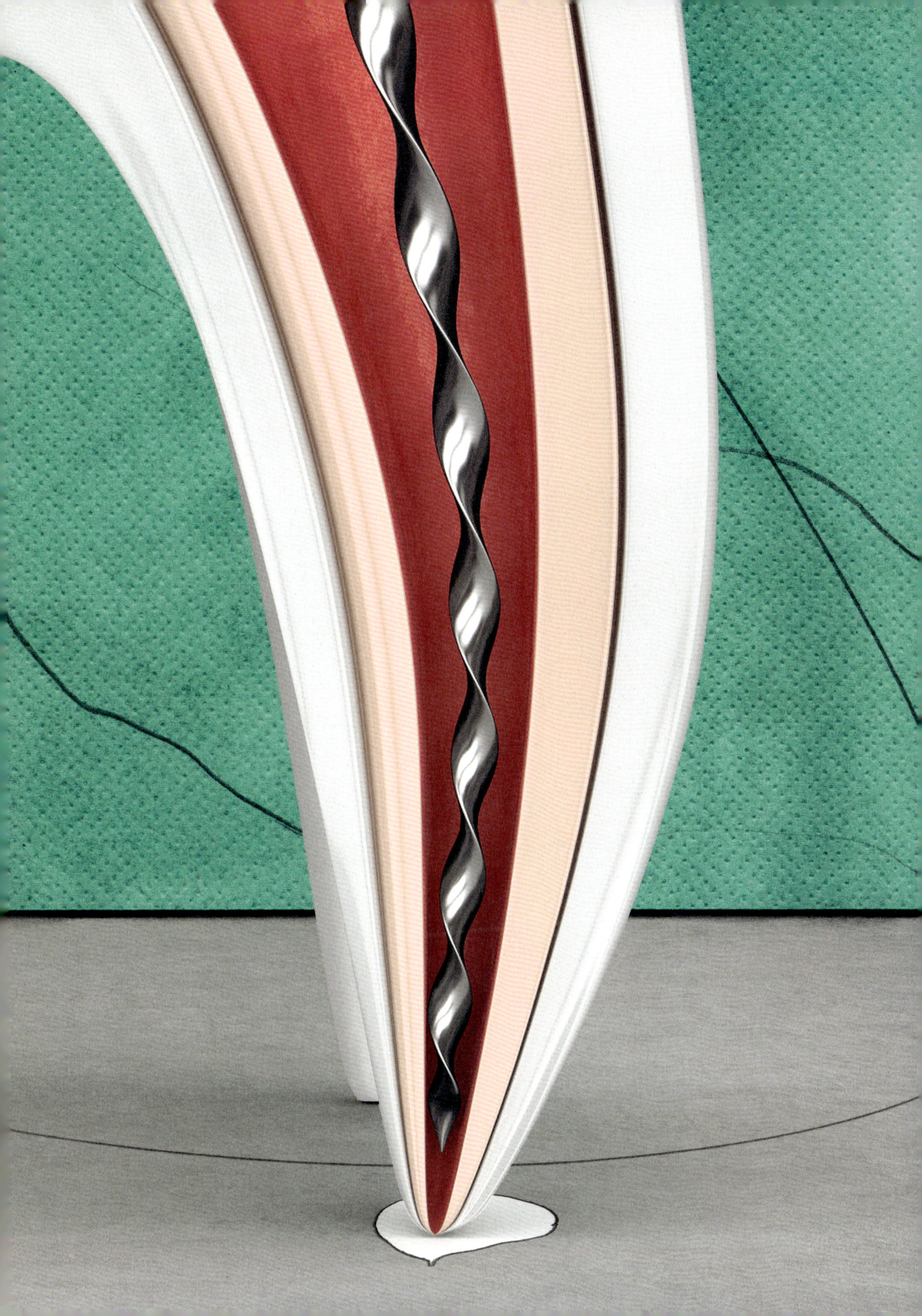

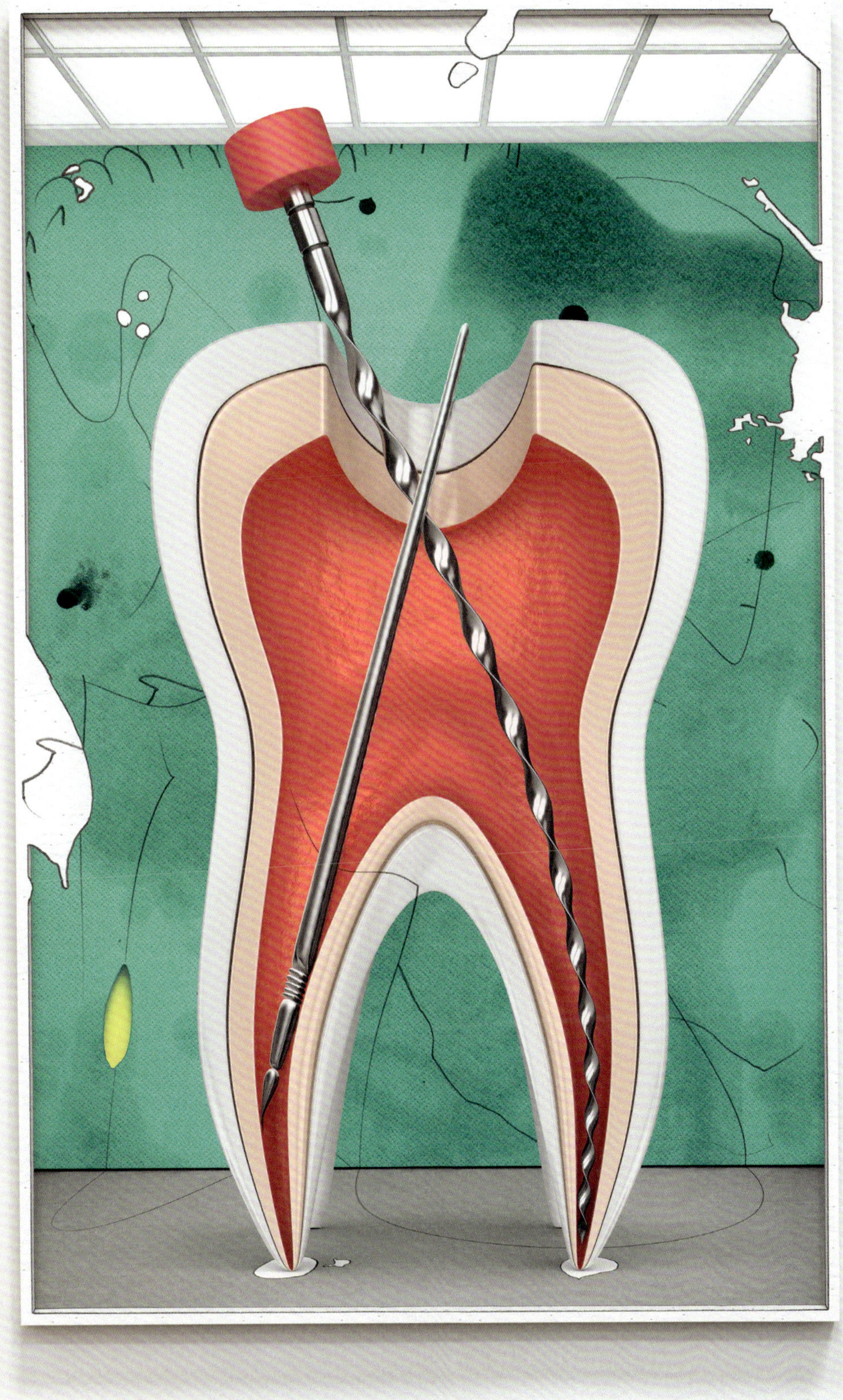

White Cube, White Teeth | 2020

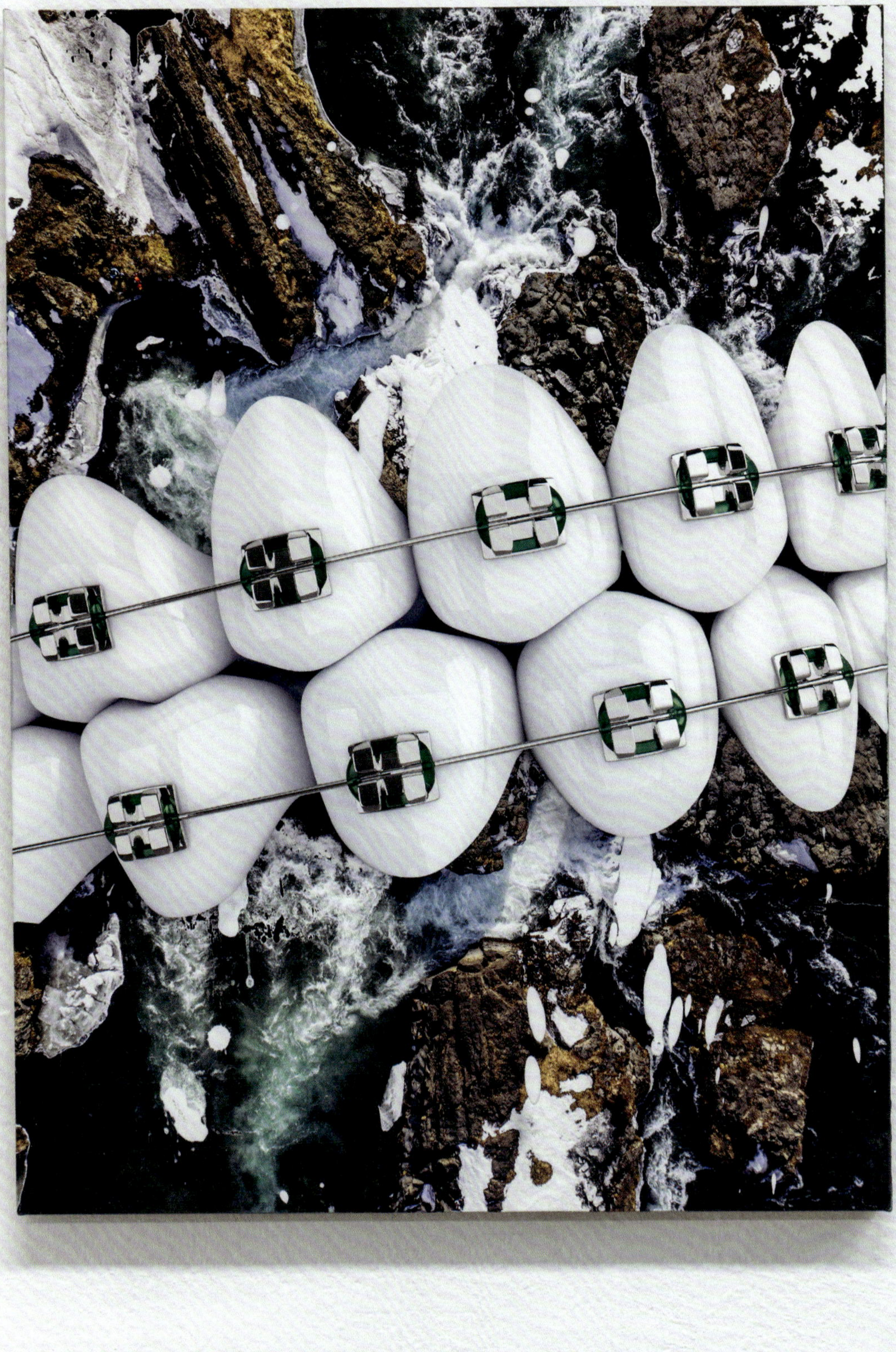

Untitled (Arctic) | 2021

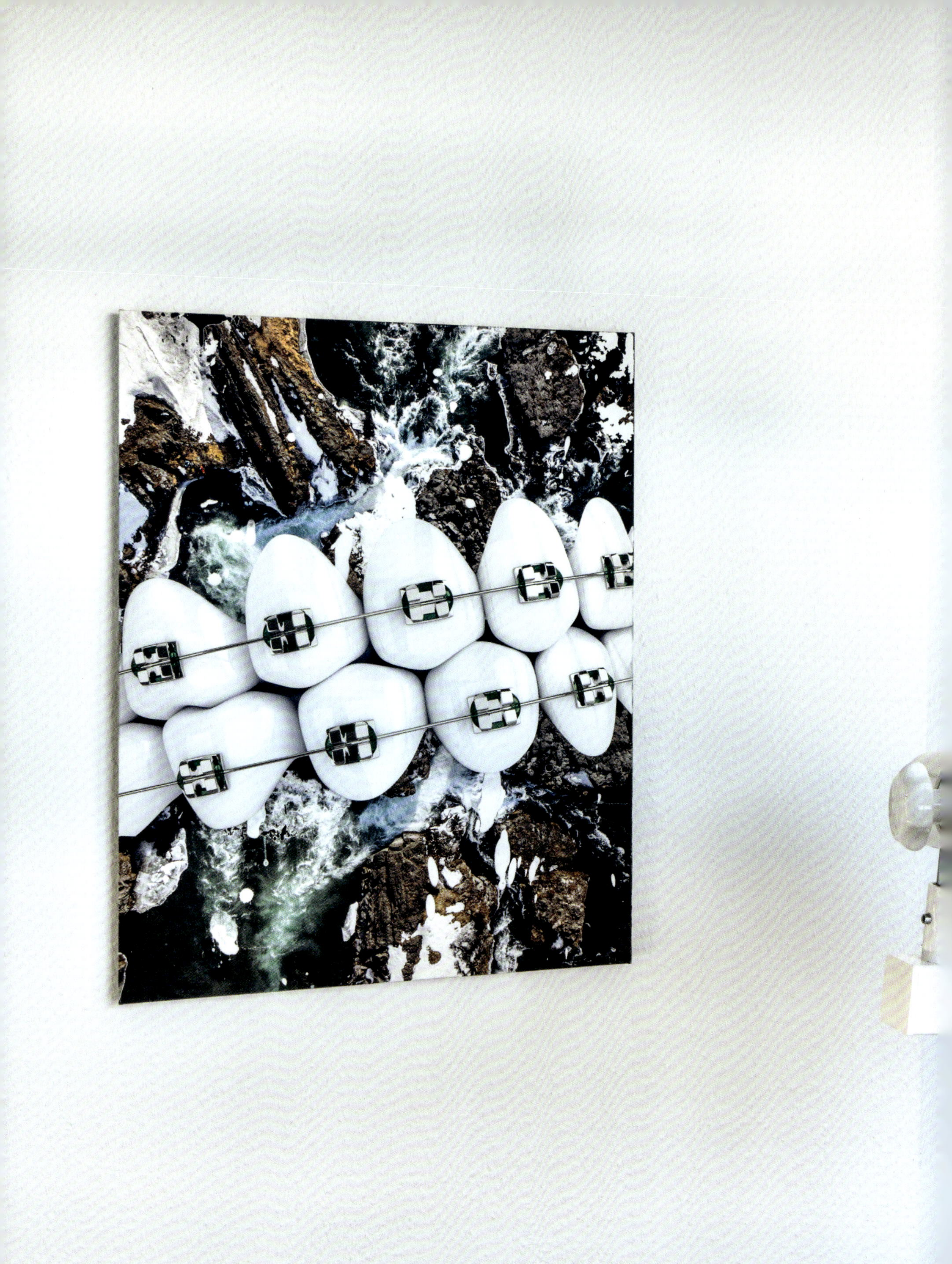

Intraoralium | Zahnarztpraxis Julia Simon | 2021

1

Untitled (bush) | Detail | 2020

3

Untitled | 2020

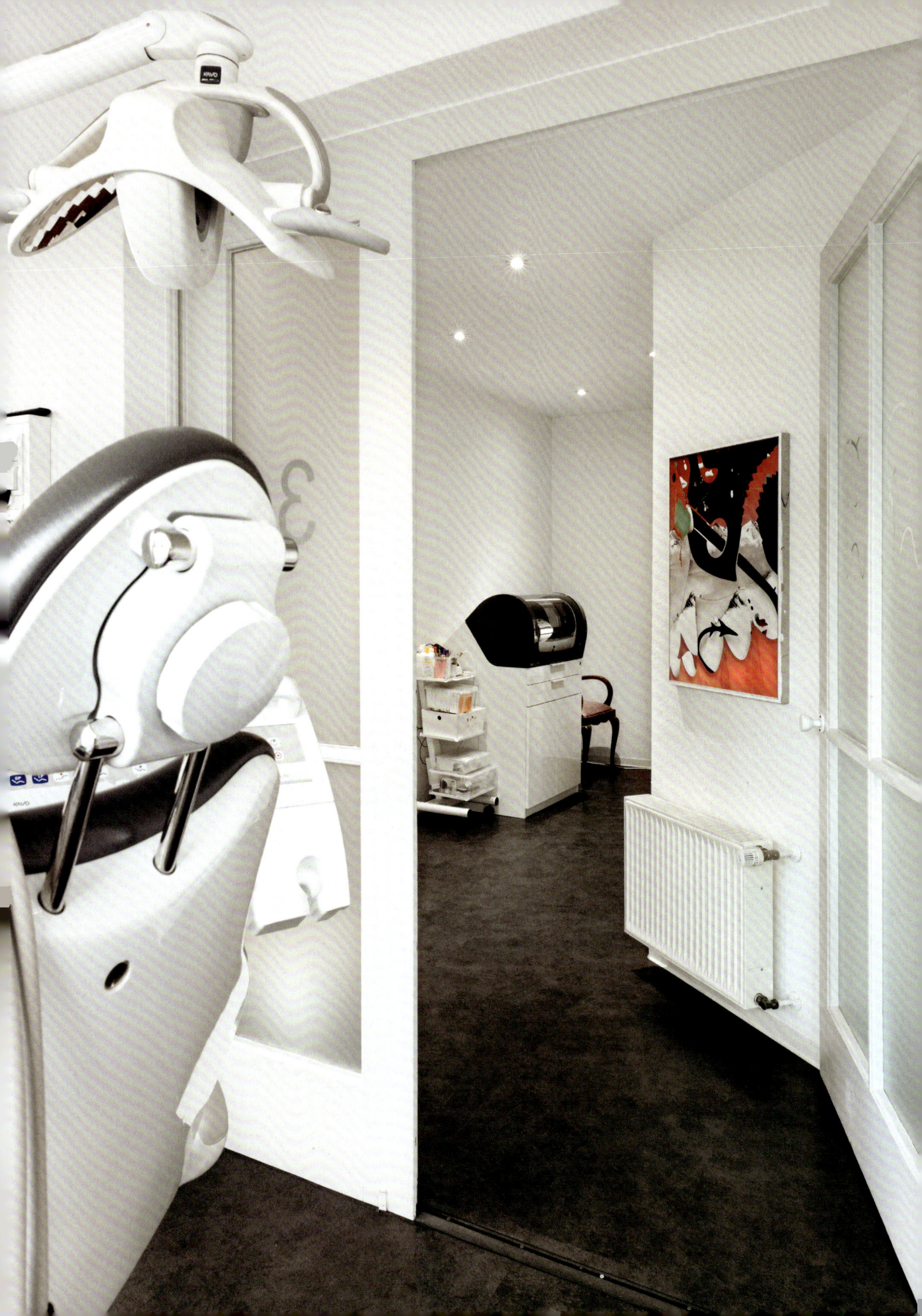

Untitled (Grandpas Visit) | 2021

Vorsicht Stufe

Untitled (sharp) | 2020

Lilian Haberer

Haarrisse und Kleckse: Zum Wiederaneignen, Übertragen und Kuratieren von Bildern

„But how does one copy-paste reality?“ [1]

In ihrem Essay über replizierte Bilddaten und 3D-Scans denkt die Künstlerin und Theoretikerin Hito Steyerl hypothetisch darüber nach, wie Bilder sich in die Objekte verwandeln könnten, die sie zeigen: wenn sie beispielsweise deren Eigenschaften annähmen. Auf 3D-Techniken bezogen, sieht sie die Bilder durch Objekte ersetzt, die wiederum auf andere Objekte verweisen, sie nicht repräsentieren, sondern replizieren. Wie lassen sich die uns vertrauten Techniken des Ausschneidens oder Kopierens und Einfügens auch darauf übertragen, was wir in der Realität und auch situativ wahrnehmen, somit replizieren können? Dies interessiert die Künstlerin im Hinblick auf dokumentarische Verfahren.

In Johannes Bendzullas Wandbildern und Bildobjekten hingegen wird diese Frage nach einer replizierten Wirklichkeit und ihren postdigitalen Bezugsobjekten (Referenten) im Bild verhandelt und durchgearbeitet. Sie wird darüber hinaus zur visuellen Erfahrungstour, zum komplexen Spiel des Zeigens und Enthüllens. In seinen Bildräumen wiederholen sich Motive und Verschachtelungen. Diese werden überlagert von hyperrealen Dingen, die mit kunstvoll geschwungenen Linien, Flecken, Spritzern, Klecksen, Haarrissen und Texturen konkurrieren. Dabei beziehen die Bilder Aufmerksamkeitsspannen und Zeitökonomien mit ein (S.37, 38). Der Prozess in Johannes Bendzullas Arbeiten ist eher ein umgekehrter, als ihn Steyerl beschreibt: Wirkliches und Alltägliches findet sich als oberflächenbearbeitete Form mit Grafikfiltern, Effekten und Schatten wieder. Auf diese Weise nehmen Alltagsdinge Eingang in die oftmals perspektivischen Raster der Räume. Dies konnte in seiner Ausstellung *#SpontexMandala* (S.80–95) nachvollzogen werden, die der Künstler 2019 in der Galerie Natalia Hug in Köln präsentierte, oder auch in der ersten Ausstellung bei Petra Rinck, Schon wieder Fühlen | Feeling Again, im selben Jahr in Düsseldorf (S.50–74).

Lilian Haberer

Hairline Cracks and Smudges: On Reappropriating, Transferring and Curating Images

„But how does one copy-paste reality?“ [1]

In her essay on replicated image data and 3D scans, the artist and theorist Hito Steyerl hypothetically considers how images might transform into the objects they depict—for example, by taking on their properties. With regard to 3D techniques, she sees images replaced by objects, which in turn reference other objects, not representing but replicating them. How can the common techniques of cutting or copying and pasting be transferred to what we perceive in reality and situationally, in order to be able to replicate it? The artist is interested in this in relation to documentary processes.

In Johannes Bendzulla's murals and pictorial objects, on the other hand, this question of a reproduced reality and its post-digital reference objects (referents) is negotiated and worked through within the image. Furthermore, it becomes a visual experiential tour, a complex game of showing and revealing. Motifs and interlaced images are duplicated in his image spaces. They are overlaid with hyper-real items that compete with artfully curved lines, flecks, splashes, blobs of paint, hairline cracks, and textures. In doing so, the images take attention spans and economies of time into account (p.37, 38). The process in Johannes Bendzulla's works is more of an inverse one than Steyerl describes: real and everyday things are found as surface-treated forms with graphic filters, effects, and shadows. In this way, everyday items make their way into the grids of the image spaces, often with perspectives. This can be observed in his exhibition *#SpontexMandala* (p. 80–95), which the artist presented at Galerie Natalia Hug in Cologne in 2019, as well as in *Schon wieder Fühlen | Feeling Again,* his first exhibition at Petra Rinck in Düsseldorf in the same year (p. 50–74).

In these shows, Johannes Bendzulla uses advertising by the company Spontex—a manufacturer of cleaning sponges and rubber gloves—in tarot card form with psychedel-

Dort hat Johannes Bendzulla die Werbung der Firma Spontex – Herstellerin von Reinigungsschwämmen und Gummihandschuhen – in Tarotkartenform mit psychedelischen Mustern und ihrem Slogan zum Anlass genommen, die auf den Tarotkarten abgebildeten Handschuhe zu Protagonistinnen seiner Bilder werden zu lassen. Während in seinen Arbeiten die gelbe Signalfarbe und noppige Oberfläche des Reinigungsarbeitsmaterials und ein farbverschmierter Gummischlauch als skulpturales Objekt dienen, ergreifen die Gegenstände und Farben auch von den cleanen Ausstellungsräumen Besitz (S.91). Es verselbständigen sich auch die Konturen der Tarotkarten über ihre dargestellten Ränder hinaus: So werden sie durch wucherndes Blattwerk überlagert, oder lassen verschiedene Materialebenen erkennen, die an Web- und Strickfasern erinnern. Handformen mit Farbverläufen lösen sich scheinbar vom Untergrund oder werden zu skulpturalen Halterungen der Karten als Displays (S.105). Die hochformatigen Inkjetprints auf Büttenpapier, das um den gesamten Rahmen gespannt ist, lassen mitunter an den Seiten gedruckte Farbschlieren erkennen. Somit dienen diese gestalteten Farbspritzer, Haarrisse und Kleckse quasi als Referenz zum gestischen Malprozess, der in *Spontex 009* als verselbständigter Pinselstrich und Schatten in Erscheinung tritt (S.53). Die Anweisung auf den zur Verfügung gestellten Tarotkarten wird zugleich mit einer lebensweltlichen Empfehlung verbunden: „Male die Karte aus und höre auf dein Herz“ oder „...und lächle“. Sie wird in Johannes Bendzullas *#SpontexMandala*-Serie von 2018 ebenfalls zum sichtbaren Motto. Dabei sind auf den Prints die Hände und Hintergründe wie Materialcollagen freigestellt vor einer Stadtsilhouette zu sehen (S.101).

Das Versprechen auf Entspannung durch Ausmalen der fünf beigefügten Kartenmotive, wie dies der Slogan von Spontex nahelegt, wird werbewirksam verwertet, indem es zusammen mit der gestalteten Karte unter dem oben genannten Hashtag hochgeladen werden kann. Selbst die Pause lässt sich noch ausgestalten und optimieren (S.77,78). Kreative Arbeit und Reinigungstätigkeit oder Hausarbeit, oftmals gar nicht oder prekär entlohnt, werden miteinander verbunden, damit instagrammable gemacht und wiederverwertet. Das schöpferische Tätigsein greift der Künstler ironisch auf, indem er Gesten und Spuren, Objekte und Motive aus der Toolbox wiederverwendet, zusammenfügt. Das vermeintlich Unverwechselbare eines Pinselstrichs oder einer Handzeichnung wird aufgegriffen, in eine digitale Signatur übersetzt, als Bildelemente zu einem Ganzen gefügt und im Druck auf Bütten als Original und Werk wiederangeeignet. Der Prozess ähnelt dabei demjenigen des Kuratierens verschiedener Bildformen und -reflektionen, die zusammengestellt und exponiert werden.

Be endlessly creative

Die Rolle des *nonstop* Schöpferisch-Aktiv-Sein-Müssens greift Johannes Bendzulla 2017 auch in seiner Einzelausstellung *XXL | XXX* für den Ausstellungsraum ≈ 5 in der U-Bahn-Passage der gleichnamigen Haltestelle am Ebertplatz in Köln auf. In einer der beiden Vitrinen stellt er den Inkjetprint „Ich kenne kein Weekend“ auf transparenter Folie in Spraypaintoptik aus. Darüber hinaus zeigt er in der anderen „24/7“, eine Installation aus Liegestühlen mit Computertastaturmotiv auf Stoff, die er vor einem Druck platziert hat. Dieser zitiert eine abstrakte Zeichnung und den auf die Vitrinenwand gesprayten Werktitel (S.241). *24/7* ist dabei das gängige Synonym für eine beständige Verfügbarkeit, Erreichbarkeit und Schlaflosigkeit, die sich aufgrund flexibilisierter Arbeitskonzepte, ständiger medialer Präsenz, digitalisierter und globalisierter Verfahren in der Produktion und Konsumption und einen 24-stündigen Dauerbetrieb auszeichnet. Jonathan Crary hat in seiner gleichnamigen Studie die Logik dieses Prinzips auf den Punkt gebracht:

ic patterns and slogans as an opportunity to allow the gloves depicted on the tarot cards become the protagonists of his images. While the hallmark yellow color and textured surface of the cleaning equipment and a paint-smeared rubber hose serve as sculptural objects in his works, the items and colors also take possession of the clean exhibition spaces (p. 91). The contours of the tarot cards also take on a life of their own beyond their depicted edges: they are overlaid by sprawling foliage, for example, or reveal different layers of material reminiscent of woven and knitted fibers. Hand shapes with color gradients are seemingly detached from the background, or become sculptural supports of the cards as displays (p.105). The portrait-format inkjet prints on handmade paper stretched around the entire frame sometimes reveal streaks of ink printed on the sides. These designed paint splatters, hairline cracks, and blobs almost serve as a reference to the gestural painting process that manifests in *Spontex_009* as independent brushstrokes and shadows (p.53). The instructions on the tarot cards provided are at the same time accompanied by everyday advice: "Color in the card and listen to your heart" or "...and smile." This is also a visible motto in Johannes Bendzulla's *#SpontexMandala* series from 2018. In these prints, the hands and backgrounds, as well as the material collages are cropped in front of a city silhouette (p.101).

The promise of relaxation through coloring in the five enclosed card motifs—as suggested by the Spontex slogan—is exploited effectively since it can be uploaded together with the completed card under the aforementioned hashtag. Even a break can still be intentionally designed and optimized (p.77, 78). Creative work and cleaning or housework, often precariously paid or not at all, are linked together, rendered Instagrammable, and re-exploited. The artist makes an ironic comment on creative activity by reusing and combining gestures, traces, objects, and motifs from the digital toolbox. The supposedly distinctive elements of a brushstroke or a hand drawing are captured, translated into a digital signature, added as pictorial elements to form a coherent whole, and reappropriated as an original work in print on handmade paper. The process resembles that of curating various pictorial forms and reflections, which are then compiled and displayed.

Be endlessly creative

Johannes Bendzulla also addressed the role of this non-stop having-to-be-creatively-active in his solo exhibition *XXL | XXX* for the exhibition space ≈ 5 in the subway passage of Ebertplatz station in Cologne in 2017. In one of the two display cases, he showed the inkjet print *Ich kenne kein Weekend (I Know No Weekend)* on transparent film in a graffiti style. In the other he displayed 24/7, an installation of deck chairs with a computer keyboard motif on their fabric that he has placed in front of a print referencing an abstract drawing and the title of the work sprayed on the wall of the exhibition vitrine (S. 241). 24/7 is a common synonym for constant availability, reachability and the end of sleep, which is characterized by flexible conceptions of work, a constant media presence, digitalized and globalized production and consumption processes, as well as a 24-hour non-stop business. In his study of the same name, Jonathan Crary succinctly summarized the logic of this principle:

> 24/7 announces a time without time, a time extracted from any material or identifiable demarcations, a time without sequence or recurrence. In its peremptory reductiveness, it celebrates a hallucination of presence [...]. [2]

This arrangement in the display cases clearly demonstrates the transparency and exposed nature of one's own creative work, during which the producer cannot afford to take

„Der Slogan propagiert eine Zeit ohne Zeit, eine Zeit, die aus allen materiellen oder bestimmbaren Umgrenzungen herausgelöst ist, eine Zeit ohne Abfolge oder Wiederholung. Ihr kategorischer Reduktionismus verherrlicht eine halluzinatorische Präsenz.“[2]

Diese Anordnung in den Vitrinen führt die Transparenz und Exponiertheit der eigenen Kreativarbeit vor Augen. Bei dieser kann sich der/die Produzent*in keine Pause leisten. Vielmehr fallen Arbeit, Freizeit und Erholung in eins und gehen in der eigenen Dauerpräsenz eines digital natives und *creative workers* auf. Die permanente Sichtbarkeit in der Vitrine mit einer zumindest suggerierten, entspannenden Sitzposition und ästhetischen Erfahrung durch die abstrakte Kunst im Hintergrund verdeutlicht auch eine mögliche, dauerhafte Überwachung:

„Die Unerbittlichkeit des Slogans 24/7 ist, bei aller Abstraktheit und Inhaltsleere, seine Zeitlosigkeit. Er ist stets Kritik und Missbilligung der Schwäche und Unzulänglichkeit menschlicher Zeit, ihrer diffusen und verschlungenen Strukturen. Er beseitigt die Bedeutung oder den Wert der Pause und der Veränderlichkeit.“[3]

Crary betont hier zwei wesentliche Aspekte dieses an Leistung orientierten Kürzels „24/7“: eine präsentische, variationslose Gegenwart und die menschliche Unfähigkeit, sich dieser Zeitlosigkeit vollständig auszuliefern. Johannes Bendzulla eignet sich in einigen seiner Werkserien und Ausstellungen eben diese mit hyperkapitalistischen Arbeits-, Erfolgs- und Kreativitätsmodellen verbundene Sprache an. Dabei reflektiert er ihre Denkstruktur und die mit ihnen verbundenen Rollenbilder, wie sie bei Berufen in der Kreativ- und Start Up-Branche, aber auch im Kunstmarkt verbreitet sind. Diesen steht andererseits ein flexibilisiertes, an Erfolgswerten ausgerichtetes, prekarisiertes Beschäftigungsverhältnis gegenüber. In seiner Ausstellung *Part One: Spring 2015 – En plein air* bei Natalia Hug beschäftigt sich Johannes Bendzulla daher mit den in der Kreativbranche vorgenommenen Vereinnahmungen von Künstler*innen als *creative workers* sowie der damit verbundenen Ökonomisierung des Outputs (S.278–297). Als Gegenbewegung zum Druck des „24/7“ und den zunehmend technologisierten Arbeitsmechanismen fungiert der seit der Industrialisierung und Digitalisierung mit neuem Leben gefüllte Topos einer Flucht in die Natur hier jedoch weder als Auszeit noch als Inspirationsquelle: auch das Sich-im-Freien-Aufhalten wird nicht als eine Referenz zum künstlerischen Malprozess *en plein air* des ausgehenden 19. Jahrhunderts verstanden. Vielmehr dient dieser Tapetenwechsel einer Flucht vor ständiger Erreichbarkeit und der eigenen Techniküberforderung: die Natur als Möglichkeit, offline zu gehen. So legt es das Statement von Leatrice Eisenman, der Kreativdirektorin des Pantone Color Institutes, in ihrem Bericht zur Frühlingssaison 2015 und die Rolle der Pantone-Farben darin nahe (S.280–281).

Dementsprechend hat Johannes Bendzulla in seinen Prints auf die sonst von ihm verwendeten werbeförmigen Bilder und die Visualisierung zugunsten einer Beschriftung und Beschreibung verzichtet: „Beautiful Young Woman Creating Sculpture“ oder „Artist Relaxing in his Studio“. Dabei handelt es sich um eine mühelose, scheinbar nebenbei entstehende kreative Produktion, sowohl durch digitale Zeichnungen vergegenwärtigt, die abstrakte gestische Formen oder digitale Farbspritzergrafiken reproduzieren und wiederholen, als auch von der Pantone-Frühlingspalette als Farbhintergründe umspielt, die in einer Creative-Designoptik umgesetzt wurden (S.289). Dieser bewusste Verzicht auf fotografische Bilder in seiner Printreihe ist konsequent; durchbrochen wird dies jedoch wieder von drei Liegestühlen als Teil der Installation, von denen zwei im hinteren Raum an der Wand befestigt, das heißt im Eingangsbereich als Objekte platziert sind. Letzteres lädt scheinbar zum Verweilen, Relaxen, zur Kontemplation vor Kunst ein. Sie sind mit dem

a break. Rather, work, free time, and rest all roll into one and merge into the distinctive permanent presence of a digital native and creative worker. The permanent visibility of the exhibition vitrine, with a relaxed sitting position—or at least implied—and the aesthetic experience provided by the abstract art in the background, also illustrates a potential permanent state of surveillance:

> In spite of its insubstantiality and abstraction as a slogan, the implacability of 24/7 is its impossible temporality. It is always a reprimand and a deprecation of the weakness and inadequacy of human time, with its blurred, meandering textures. It effaces the relevance or value of any respite or variability.[3]

Here Crary points out two essential aspects of this performance-oriented abbreviation 24/7: a presentist, unvarying now, and the human inability to fully surrender to this impossible temporality. In some of his work series and exhibitions, Johannes Bendzulla appropriates this exact language associated with hypercapitalist models of work, success, and creativity. In doing so, he reflects on the structure of their ideas and their associated role models that are prevalent in professions in the creative and start-up industries, but also in the art market. In contrast, there is a flexible, precarious employment oriented toward success values. In his exhibition Part One: *Spring 2015—En plein air* at Natalia Hug, Johannes Bendzulla explored the appropriation of artists as creative workers in the creative industry and the associated economization of output (p. 278 – 297). However, the trope of an escape into nature as a countermovement to the pressure of 24/7 and increasingly technologized work mechanisms, filled with new life since the age of industrialization and digitalization, acts here neither as a time-out nor as a source of inspiration: time spent outside is also not understood as a reference to the *en plein air* painting practice of the late nineteenth century. Rather, this change of scenery serves as an escape from constant reachability and one's own technological overload: nature as an opportunity to go offline. This is suggested by a statement by Leatrice Eisenman, creative director of the Pantone Color Institute, in her report on the 2015 spring season and the role played by Pantone colors (p. 280 – 281).

Johannes Bendzulla has accordingly dispensed with the advertising-style imagery and visualization usually present in his prints in favor of caption and description: *Beautiful Young Woman Creating Sculpture or Artist Relaxing in his Studio*. This is an effortless, seemingly incidental creative production, realized both through digital drawings that reproduce and repeat abstract gestural forms or digital paint splash graphics, as well as the use of the Pantone spring palette as the surrounding color backgrounds to give a creative design look (S. 289). This deliberate renunciation of photographic images in his print series is consistent, although this is interrupted once again by three deck chairs forming part of the installation, two of which are attached to the wall in the back room, that is, placed as objects in the entrance area. The latter seemingly invites the viewer to linger, to relax, to contemplate the art. They are printed with an edited stock photo and show a half-length image or portrait of a young woman in a skimpy dress outdoors. The strokes created with a palette and brush were added using Photoshop.

The fact that these strategies of reappropriation and ironic exaggeration are not fully convincing in all aspects becomes clear here: counter-images and gestures, rather than sometimes an ironic and critical attitude only, are required to counter the power of these banal advertising images, which also often fall back on sexist stereotypes. The ironic instrumentalization of the slogans "Sex sells" and "Size Matters" is directed at the immaterial form of the economization of knowledge and thought for an attention economy, whose principles govern Johannes Bendzulla's choice of poster motif for the aforementioned

bearbeiteten Stockfoto bedruckt und zeigen eine Außenaufnahme als Halbfigur oder das Porträt einer jungen Frau im knappen Kleid. Die mit Palette und Pinsel erzeugten Striche wurden per Photoshop hinzugefügt.

Dass die Strategien der Wiederaneignung und ironischen Überspitzung nicht in allen Aspekten überzeugen, wird hier deutlich: Für die Macht der banalen, aber auch oftmals auf sexistische Stereotype zurückgreifenden Werbebilder bedarf es mitunter mehr als einer ironisch-kritischen Haltung, sondern vielmehr der Gegenbilder und -gesten. Die ironische Instrumentalisierung der Slogans „Sex sells“ und „Size Matters“ für eine Aufmerksamkeitsökonomie, nach deren Prinzip Johannes Bendzulla sein Plakatmotiv für die zuvor beschriebene Ausstellung am Kölner Ebertplatz ausgesucht hat – ein endlos langer, umgedrehter Lackstiefel mit den massiven 3D-Buchstaben des Titels *XXL | XXX* –, richtet sich auf die immaterielle Form der Ökonomisierung von Wissen und Denken (Abb. Nächste Seite links). Im Unterschied zu neoliberalen, globalisierten Ökonomien, die sich räumlich auswirkten, prägen Formen des kognitiven Kapitalismus und damit verbundene Machtdynamiken Verstand und Denken. Diese konfigurieren somit zeitliche Strukturen mit und stellten eine Verbindung zu Gedächtnis und Aufmerksamkeit her, wie es Deborah Hauptmann auf den Punkt bringt. Die Produktion konzentriere sich somit nicht mehr auf rein materielle Produkte, sondern auf immaterielle Verbindungen, denen die Kräfte von *bios* und *nous* (Körper und Geist) durch Biopolitik und Noopolitik[4] ausgesetzt sind, quasi als Humankapital, das sich auf die menschliche und vor allem geistig-kreative Arbeitskraft bezieht.

Angela McRobbie hat in ihrem Buch *Be Creative* den Charakter dieser neuen Kreativindustrien beschrieben. Sie betrachtet die damit einhergehenden Arbeitsformen von Selbständigkeit, Freelancing, die kreative und künstlerische Arbeit zunehmend prägen, und fasst zusammen: „The seemingly exciting compensation for work without protection is the personal reward of ‚being creative‘.“[5] In ihrer Analyse wiegt der immaterielle Wert des Kreativseins oftmals das ungesicherte Arbeitsverhältnis auf. Auch in der Entwicklung der sogenannten *Creative Industries* zeigt sich eine veränderte Struktur: Hierbei handelt es sich eben nicht mehr um Großbetriebe oder -unternehmen, sondern vielmehr um „Pseudo-Institutionen“, um projektbasierte Cluster unabhängiger Produzent*innen, wie Gerald Raunig betont.[6]

Auch eine frühere Serie Bendzullas, „Art Business as usual – real whiteboards“, widmet sich genau diesem neuen Bild einer kreativen Umgebung in Form von solchen in Firmen, Agenturen und Start-Ups verwendeten Tafeln für den kreativen Prozess und Austausch. Medienassemblagen und whiteboards, die hier mit Folienmarkerlinien, Diagrammen und Formen beschrieben waren, wurden zusammen mit Drucken von Stockfotografien im Kunstverein Düsseldorf ausgestellt (S. 210 – 223). Die Fotos zeigen Werbeaufnahmen inszenierter und symbolhafter Arbeitssituationen, wie sie als Stockfotografien vielfach für vorgefertigte Broschüren und Powerpoint- oder Keynote-Präsentationen vorgesehen sind. Der Künstler hat sich in viele der *role models* mit demselben Selbstporträt und somit dem immer gleichen stoischen Gesichtsausdruck hineinmontiert. So spielt er das Narrativ des Business-Künstlers mit Tagebucheinträgen als Kommentare zu den Fotos und seine verschiedenen Rollen und Funktionen durch: als erfolgreicher Geschäftsmann mit Aktenkoffer und Anzug, als internationaler Geschäftspartner, als Teamleiter im Hintergrund, in der Rolle des Moderators. Er zeigt sich jedoch auch in seinen eigenen Darstellungen als einer derjenigen, die buchstäblich die eigene skulpturale Profitpfeilskulptur der Firma ziehen oder selbst auf der höchsten Stele einer 3D-Wachstumsgrafik stehen, die einer minimalistischen Rauminstallation ähnelt (S. 218 – 219 & S. 222 – 223). Hier kommt zum Tragen, was Paolo Virno bereits in seiner *Grammatik der Multitude* als Charakteristik dieser Industrien beschrieben hatte, dass es vor allem um eine kommunikative „Tätigkeit ohne Werk“ gehe.[7] Der Künstler ist

Invitation / Einladungskarte XXL | XXX | 2017

exhibition at Cologne's Ebertplatz—an endlessly long, upside-down patent leather boot with the enormous 3D letters of the title *XXL | XXX* (fig. above). In contrast to neoliberal, globalized economies that operate spatially, forms of cognitive capitalism and associated power dynamics shape our ideas and understanding. These in turn reconfigure temporal structures and establish a link to memory and attention, as Deborah Hauptmann neatly summarizes. She argues that production is no longer focused on purely material products, but on intangible connections that govern the forces of bios and nous (body and mind) through biopolitics and noopolitics,[4] as a form of human capital relating to a workforce of people that are cognitive and creative above all else.

Vermarkter und Vermittler, sein Werk sind die Wachstumsversprechungen des Unternehmens, des Outputs und der Kreativität, die er abbildet. Sein Gesicht wird zur Marke, das, unendlich reproduziert, sich warenförmig in die Rhetorik der Optimierung einpassen lässt.

In dem Beharren auf einer faltenlosen Homogenität der Kleidung und Gesichter sowie der damit verbundenen heteronormativen Menschen- und Körperbilder in den durchgespielten Bürosituationen mit cleanen Innenräumen reproduzieren die Bilder Modellformen und Stereotype einer kritisierten Kulturindustrie als Struktur sozialer und kapitalistischer Repression. Die *Creative Industries* von heute sind in ihrer hybridisierten, kommerzialisierten Produktion gemäß Ulf Wuggenig – der die verschiedenen Konjunkturen des Kreativitätsbegriffs beleuchtet hat – dabei, high und low miteinander zu verbinden, Kultur zu demokratisieren, aber vor allem: sich der Effekte des Wachstums im kulturellen Sektor bewusst zu sein.[8]

Insofern arbeitet Johannes Bendzulla gezielt auch hier mit einem Überschuss, einem Zuviel dieser Gebrauchsfotografie, -grafik und Ästhetik. Er fordert diesen einen Kippmoment heraus und beschreitet damit einen schmalen Grat, auf dem diese geglätteten und uns täglich in der Öffentlichkeit umspülenden Displays allgegenwärtig sind und wiederbegegnen: im urbanen Raum, in analogen, digitalen oder sozialen Medien, durch Wiederaneignung, Übersetzung und das Kuratieren der mit ihnen verbundenen Formate. Im Ausstellungsraum oder in der privatwirtschaftlichen Galerie schmiegen sich diese Arbeiten eben nicht nur an die exponierte Logik der Bilder an, sondern sie lassen dieselben durchlässig für Verflechtungen, *entganglements* werden und zeigen ihre Verstrickungen.

Indem er als Kurator und Kommentator dieser Bilder und Gesten auftritt, sie in einer digitalen, von Grafikfiltern, Farbpaletten, den spezifischen Formaten, ihren Formatierungen und Zurichtungen geprägten Umgebung verhandelt, verwandelt Johannes Bendzulla die Sprache der bereits von Félix Guattari prognostizierten postmedialen Zeit und ihrer „kollektiven-individuellen Wiederaneignung“[9] an.

„Das Motiv für Realismus ist nie Bestätigung der Wirklichkeit, sondern Protest.“[10]

Dieser prägnante Satz von Alexander Kluge aus seinen Schriften zur „realistischen Methode“, die er auf den Film bezog, ist ein Plädoyer für das sinnliche Erleben der Filmschaffenden und Filmsehenden. Dies hieße für sie, sich im Medium Film gegen die Wirklichkeit aufzulehnen, daran zu arbeiten, was für sie Realität bedeutet, Zusammenhänge herzustellen und sich dieser heterogenen, polyphonen Wirklichkeit zu stellen.[11] Kluge ist in seiner Filmkunst ein Vertreter der Montage und des Samplings, er regt in seinen Filmen und Schriften das Aktivieren des inneren Films an, der sich gegenüber einer reinen Repräsentation behauptet.

Um die sinnliche, taktile Wahrnehmung geht es auch in den Displays und Ausstellungsgestaltungen Johannes Bendzullas, die vom Plakat über die Anordnung und Inszenierung der Arbeiten im Ausstellungsraum Teil einer eigenen, inneren filmischen Wahrnehmung werden. Durch die Ablösung der Bilder von ihren Referenten wird die Betrachtung von Wirklichkeit und die Konfrontation mit dieser zu einer subjektiven Erfahrung. Durch Irritationsmomente in den Bildern, die mit Spuren, Fehlstellen, variablen Größenverhältnissen und Überschreitungen von Rändern arbeiten, entstehen subtile Realitätsverschiebungen. Diese werden anhand einer frühen Einladungskarte für das Grafische Kabinett Düsseldorf deutlich: Sie führen die medialen Samplingprozesse wie auch das Spiel mit Wahrnehmung und Wirklichkeitserfahrung anschaulich vor Augen (Abbildung nächste Seite rechts).

Die Einladung zeigt ein weitgehend leeres Blatt, nur in der Mitte befindet sich eine geschweifte Klammer, wie von einer Schreibmaschine getippt. Darunter, etwas weiter rechts von der Mitte, ist der Tierkörper einer toten Stechmücke zu sehen, die auf dem

Angela McRobbie has described the character of these new creative industries in her book *Be Creative.* She looks at the associated work forms of self-employment and freelancing, which are increasingly coming to characterize creative and artistic work, and summarizes: "The seemingly exciting compensation for work without protection is the personal reward of 'being creative.'"[5] In her analysis, the intangible value of being creative often outweighs an insecure employment relationship. The development of the so-called creative industries also reflects a change in the structure: they are no longer large companies or enterprises, but rather "pseudo-institutions," project-based clusters of independent producers, as Gerald Raunig points out.[6]

An earlier series by Bendzulla, *Art Business as usual—real whiteboards,* is also devoted to this new image of a creative environment in the form of companies, agencies and start-ups using these boards for the creative process and sharing ideas. Media samplings and whiteboards drawn with permanent marker lines, diagrams and shapes were exhibited together with prints of stock photographs at the Kunstverein Düsseldorf (p.210–223). The photographs depict publicity shots of staged and symbolic work situations, for these stock photographs are often provided to design prefabricated brochures and PowerPoint or Keynote presentations. The artist has edited himself into many of these role models with the same self-portrait and therefore permanently stoic facial expression. He plays out the narrative of the business artist with diary entries commenting the photos as well as his various other roles and functions: as a successful businessman in a suit with a briefcase, as an international business partner, as a team leader in the background, as a moderator. However, he also appears in his own depictions as someone who is literally pulling the company's own sculptural profit arrow or places himself on the highest bar of a 3D growth graphic that resembles a minimalist installation (S.218–219 & S.222–223). What comes into play here is what Paolo Virno had already described as a characteristic of these industries in his *Grammar of the Multitude,* that it is first and foremost a communicative "non-productive labor."[7] The artist is a marketer and mediator; his works are promises of growth, of the business, the output, and the creativity that he represents. His face becomes a brand that, infinitely reproduced, can be commodified to fit the rhetoric of optimization.

In the insistence on an unwrinkled homogeneity of clothing and faces, as well as the associated heteronormative images of people and bodies in the reenacted office situations with clean interiors, the images reproduce model forms and stereotypes of a criticized culture industry as a structure of social and capitalist repression. According to Ulf Wuggenig, who has shed light on the various economies of the concept of creativity, today's creative industries, with their hybridized, commercialized production, are in the process of combining high and low, of democratizing culture, but—first and foremost—of being aware of the effects of growth in the cultural sector.[8]

In this respect, Johannes Bendzulla is also deliberately working with a surplus here, an excess of commercial photography, graphics, and aesthetics. He challenges this overturning moment and treads a fine line where these smoothed displays that wash over us in the public sphere on a daily basis are ubiquitous and re-encountered: in urban space, in analog, digital, or social media, through re-appropriation, translation, and the curation of the formats associated with them. Whether in an exhibition space or a private gallery, these works not only cling to the exposed logic of the images, but allow the same to become permeable to interrelations and entanglements while revealing their enmeshments.

By acting as a curator and commentator of these images and gestures, negotiating them in a digital environment characterized by graphic filters, color palettes, specific sizes, formatting and adjustments, Johannes Bendzulla adopts the language of the post-media era and its "collective-individual re-appropriation" as diagnosed by Félix Guattari.[9]

Invitation | Einladungskarte | Grafisches Kabinett Düsseldorf | 2012

Blatt mit dem Kopf und Rüssel dicht an der Papieroberfläche festzustecken scheint, beide Bildobjekte sind in Originalgröße abgebildet. Da sie eine fotografische Aufnahme dieses Arrangements zeigt, stellt sich eine Verunsicherung durch das Ineinanderschieben zweier Zeitebenen ein: Der kurze Augenblick dieses Zusammentreffens wurde über das Verteilen und Verschicken unendlich oft reproduziert und zu einer dauerhaften Konstellation. Dann gerät auch der eigene Blick in den Fokus. Denn der Raum des vermeintlichen Blattes ist unklar, da sich die abstrakte Klammer und das Tier mit Schatten auf unterschiedlichen Ebenen zu befinden scheinen. Und eine weitere Frage stellt sich ein: Ob es sich bei dem perspektivisch wahrgenommenen Tier nicht von vornherein um eine Bilddatei handelt, die per Copy and Paste eingesetzt und bearbeitet wurde, so dass alle Materialität vermittelnde Qualitäten sichtbar werden?

Dass es sich bei der Einladungskarte zu Johannes Bendzullas Ausstellung im Grafischen Kabinett Düsseldorf 2012 um ein Trompe-l'œil handelt, wird unmittelbar deutlich, da sich die Aufmerksamkeit auf die Betrachtung und die Irritation des Auges verlagert hat, bei der die Mücke als Bildzeichen und damit der Bildraum als Teil unserer Realität behauptet wird. Dabei war und ist das sehr vertraute Spiel mit der Darstellung und ihrer Ähnlichkeit zu Wirklichem in der Kunst weithin bekannt. Die Verstiegenheit, haptisch greifbare Dinge darzustellen, neben einer behaupteten naturalistischen Vergegenwärtigung der Malerei, wie dies in barocken Stillleben gemalte Früchte und Fliegen bewerkstelligen, lässt einerseits an die Täuschung verschiedener Lebewesen bis hin zu den Rezipient*innen

"The motive for realism is never the confirmation of reality but protest."[10]

This incisive sentence by Alexander Kluge, from his writings on the "realistic method" as it pertained to film, is a plea for a sensory experience for both filmmakers and film viewers. For them, he contends, this would mean revolting against reality through the medium of film, working on what reality means to them, joining the dots, and facing this heterogeneous, polyphonic reality.[11] In his film art, Kluge is an advocate of montage and sampling; in his films and writing, he encourages the activation of the inner film, which asserts itself against pure representation.

Johannes Bendzulla's displays and exhibition designs are also concerned with sensory, tactile perception; from the poster to the arrangement and staging of the works in the exhibition space, all become part of their own inner cinematic perception. Through the detachment of the images from their referents, the viewing of reality and the confrontation with it becomes a subjective experience. Subtle shifts in reality are produced through disorientating moments in the images, which are created through traces, imperfections, variable proportions, and exceeding the edges. They become clear in an early invitation for the Grafisches Kabinett Düsseldorf, where they vividly demonstrate media sampling processes as well as an experimentation with perception and the experience of reality (p.45, previous page, left).

The invitation is a largely empty sheet of paper, with only a curly bracket in the center, as if typed by a typewriter. Below it, a little further to the right of center, is the carcass of a dead mosquito, which appears to be stuck fast to the surface of the paper by its head and mouth; both pictorial objects are reproduced in their original size. Since it features a photographic image of this arrangement, an uncertainty is established through the collision of two temporal planes: the brief moment of this encounter has been endlessly reproduced via distribution and mailing, becoming a permanent configuration. Then one's own gaze also comes into focus, for the space of the illusory sheet of paper is unclear, since the abstract bracket and the animal with a shadow appear to be on different levels. And another question arises: whether this three-dimensional animal is not in the first place an image file that has been inserted by copy and paste and edited so that all the qualities mediating its materiality have been rendered visible?

The fact that the invitation to Johannes Bendzulla's exhibition at the Grafisches Kabinett Düsseldorf 2012 is a trompe-l'œil becomes immediately clear, for the reader's attention is deflected to the contemplation and disorientation of the eye, in which the mosquito is asserted as a visual symbol and with it the pictorial space as part of our reality. What's more, this familiar manipulation of representation and its resemblance to reality was and is still widely prominent in art. The eccentricity of depicting haptically tangible things along with a purportedly naturalistic painting, like the fruit and flies of baroque still lifes, makes us think on the one hand of the deception of different beings, right up to the recipients of the invitations themselves—and thus illustrates the tension of the ancient contest between Zeuxis and Parrhasios. On the other hand, the poster also refers to the temporality of the scene. Yet the irony is that this insect no longer testifies to life and its transitory nature, for it is no longer alive, and the curly bracket with the blank space is also nothing more than a reference to something that is absent.

Nicholas Mirzoeff also points out that this visual game contributes less to deception than to clarifying how we see and what we perceive, when he describes seeing as a process of change and adaptation that can be trained through optical games. Mirzoeff thus attributes an essential role to the brain, whose processes and mechanisms are transmitted through such visual experiments.[12] Johannes Bendzulla, however, goes in a different direction with his arrangement, since the pictorial objects in the digital black-and-white

selbst denken – und führt damit vor Augen, was die Spannung des antiken Wettstreits zwischen Zeuxis und Parrhasios ausmacht. Andererseits verweist das Plakat auf die Zeitlichkeit der Szene. Doch die Ironie ist, dass das Insekt hier nicht mehr zur bezeugenden Instanz des Lebens und seiner Veränderung wird, da es nicht mehr lebt und auch die geschweifte Klammer mit der Leerstelle nur auf etwas verweist, was abwesend ist.

Dass dieses visuelle Spiel weniger zur Täuschung beiträgt als zur Verdeutlichung dazu, wie wir sehen und was wir wahrnehmen, betont auch Nicholas Mirzoeff, wenn er das Sehen als einen Prozess der Veränderung und Anpassung beschreibt. Dieses könne über optische Spiele geschult werden. Mirzoeff spricht damit dem Gehirn einen wesentlichen Anteil zu, dessen Abläufe und Mechanismen sich bei solchen Sehexperimenten vermitteln.[12] Johannes Bendzulla verleiht seinem Arrangement jedoch eine andere Wendung, da die Bildobjekte im digitalen Schwarz-Weiß-Foto als Datensätze zusammenkommen, aber auch als virtuelle Erscheinungen nur eine *ghostly presence* aufweisen. In seiner künstlerischen Arbeit zeigt sich das Virtuelle als eine Auseinandersetzung und ein informiertes Spiel mit Techniken und Technologien des Bildes. Dazu fungiert es als ein Befragen seiner Potenzialität. „Im Virtuellen differiert das Reale"[13] und ist somit dem Realen nicht entgegengesetzt. Es aktualisiert sich vielmehr im Prozess. So lassen die Virtualitäten der digitalen Bilder sich nicht als „Reduktionen des Realen" verstehen, sondern eröffnen „neue Matrizen der Wahrnehmung".[14]

In den Arbeiten Johannes Bendzullas erscheint das Virtuelle als Ort, an dem die heterogenen, digital erzeugten und bearbeiteten Erscheinungen zusammenkommen und es anhand der vielfachen, wenn auch nur digital konstruierten Texturen, der mit Büttenpapier umhüllten Prints und der aufgesetzten Rahmen an eine zumeist visuell vermittelte Materialität rückgebunden wird. Seine Verfahren der Wiederaneignung, Übersetzung und Zusammenstellung dieser differenten Spuren des Realen aktualisieren sich durch die Erfahrung im Ausstellungsraum.

1 Hito Steyerl, „Ripping Reality: Blind Spots and Wrecked Data in 3D", in: dies., *Duty Free Art*, London/New York 2017, S. 191–w205, hier S. 191.

2 Jonathan Crary, *24/7. Schlaflos im Spätkapitalismus*, Berlin 2014, S. 31.

3 Ebd.

4 Deborah Hauptmann, „Introduction: Architecture & Mind in the Age of Communication and Information", in: dies./Warren Neidich (Hg.), *Cognitive Architecture. From Biopolitics to Noopolitics. Architecture & Mind in the Age of Communication and Information*, Rotterdam 2010, S. 10–43, hier S. 35.

5 Angela McRobbie, *Be Creative. Making a Living in the New Culture Industries*, Cambridge Mass. 2016, S. 13.

6 Gerald Raunig, „Kreativindustrie als Massenbetrug", in: ders./Ulf Wuggenig (Hg.), *Kritik der Kreativität*, Wien 2016, S. 167–186, hier S. 179.

7 Paolo Virno, *Grammatik der Multitude. Untersuchung zu gegenwärtigen Lebensformen*, Berlin 2005, S. 50 [*Grammatica della moltitudine. Per una analisi delle forme di vita contemporanee*, Milano 2003].

8 Vgl. Ulf Wuggenig, „Heute – 1968 – 1950. Über die Höhen und Tiefen des Kreativitätsbegriffs", in: *Kunstforum International* 250 (2017), S. 102–115. Siehe auch Ulf Wuggenig, „Kreativitätsbegriffe", in: ders./Raunig 2016 Anm. 6, S. 11–69, hier S. 47–48.

9 Félix Guattari, „Towards a Post-Media Era", in: Clemens Apprich/Josephine Berry Slater/Anthony Iles/Oliver Lerone Schultz (Hg.), *Provocative Alloys:* A Post-Media Anthology, Lüneburg 2013, S. 26–27, hier S. 27.

10 Alexander Kluge, „Die schärfste Ideologie: daß die Realität sich auf ihren realistischen Charakter beruft", in: ders., *Gelegenheitsarbeit einer Sklavin. Zur realistischen Methode*, Frankfurt am Main 1978, S. 214–221, hier S. 216.

11 Vgl. auch Eike Wenzel, „Die radikale Utopie von Kluges Knie", in: taz, 6.01.2000, https://taz.de/!1254751/ (Stand: 25.01.2021).

12 *Nicholas Mirzoeff, How to See the World. An Introduction to Images from Self-Portraits, Selfies, Maps to Movies, and More*, New York 2016, S. 80 f.

13 Hans-Joachim Lenger/Michaela Ott/Sarah Speck/Harald Strauß, „Vorwort", in: dies. (Hg.), *Virtualität + Kontrolle*, Hamburg 2010, S. 6–22, hier S. 20.

14 Éric Alliez/Elisabeth von Samsonow, *Telenoia. Kritik der virtuellen Bilder*, Wien 1999, S. 9.

photograph come together as data sets, but even as virtual phenomena they only manifest a ghostly presence. In his artistic work, the virtual appears as an exploration and informed experimentation with the techniques and technologies of the image. It also functions as an interrogation of its potentiality. "In the virtual, the real is different,"[13] and so it is therefore not opposed to the real. Rather, it is brought into the present reality (is actualized) through the process. Consequently, the virtualities of digital images cannot be understood as "reductions of the real," but instead open up "new matrices of perception."[14]

In Johannes Bendzulla's works, the virtual emerges as a place where heterogeneous, digitally generated and processed appearances come together and are embedded in a largely visually mediated materiality by means of the multiple—if only digital—textures, the prints surrounded by handmade paper, and the superimposed frames. His processes of reappropriating, translating, and composing these different traces of the real are brought into the present reality through the experience in the exhibition space.

1 Hito Steyerl, "Ripping Reality: Blind Spots and Wrecked Data in 3D," in: *Hito Steyerl, Duty Free Art*, London/New York 2017, pp. 191–205, here p. 191.
2 Jonathan Crary, *24/7: Late Capitalism and the Ends of Sleep*, London/New York 2013, p. 29.
3 Ibid.
4 Deborah Hauptmann, "Introduction: Architecture & Mind in the Age of Communication and Information," in: Deborah Hauptmann/Warren Neidich (eds.), *Cognitive Architecture. From Biopolitics to Noopolitics. Architecture & Mind in the Age of Communication and Information,* Rotterdam 2010, pp. 10–43, here p. 35.
5 Angela McRobbie, *Be Creative. Making a Living in the New Culture Industries,* Cambridge Mass. 2016, p. 13.
6 Gerald Raunig, "Kreativindustrie als Massenbetrug," in: Gerald Raunig/Ulf Wuggenig (eds.), *Kritik der Kreativität*, Vienna 2016, pp. 167–186, here p. 179.
7 Paolo Virno, *A Grammar of the Multitude: For an Analysis of Contemporary Forms of Life*, Cambridge 2004, p. 54 *[Grammatica della moltitudine. Per una analisi delle forme di vita contemporanee,* Milano 2003].
8 See Ulf Wuggenig, "Heute–1968–1950. Über die Höhen und Tiefen des Kreativitätsbegriffs," in: *Kunstforum International* 250 (2017), pp. 102–115. See also Ulf Wuggenig, "Kreativitätsbegriffe," in: Wuggenig/Raunig 2016, note 6, pp. 11–69, here pp. 47–48.
9 Félix Guattari, "Towards a Post-Media Era," in: Clemens Apprich/Josephine Berry Slater/Anthony Iles/Oliver Lerone Schultz (eds.), *Provocative Alloys: A Post-Media Anthology,* Lüneburg 2013, pp. 26–27, here p. 27.
10 Alexander Kluge, "Die schärfste Ideologie: daß die Realität sich auf ihren realistischen Charakter beruft," in: Alexander Kluge, *Gelegenheitsarbeit einer Sklavin. Zur realistischen Methode,* Frankfurt am Main 1978, pp. 214–221, here p. 216.
11 See also Eike Wenzel, "Die radikale Utopie von Kluges Knie," in: taz, 6.1.2000, https://taz.de/!1254751/ (last accessed: 25.01.2021).
12 Nicholas Mirzoeff, *How to See the World. An Introduction to Images from Self-Portraits, Selfies, Maps to Movies, and More,* New York 2016, p. 80 f.
13 Hans-Joachim Lenger/Michaela Ott/Sarah Speck/Harald Strauß, "Vorwort," in: Lenger/Ott/Speck/Strauß (eds.), *Virtualität + Kontrolle*, Hamburg 2010, pp. 6–22, here p. 20.
14 Éric Alliez/Elisabeth von Samsonow, *Telenoia. Kritik der virtuellen Bilder*, Vienna 1999, p. 9.

Schon Wieder Fühlen

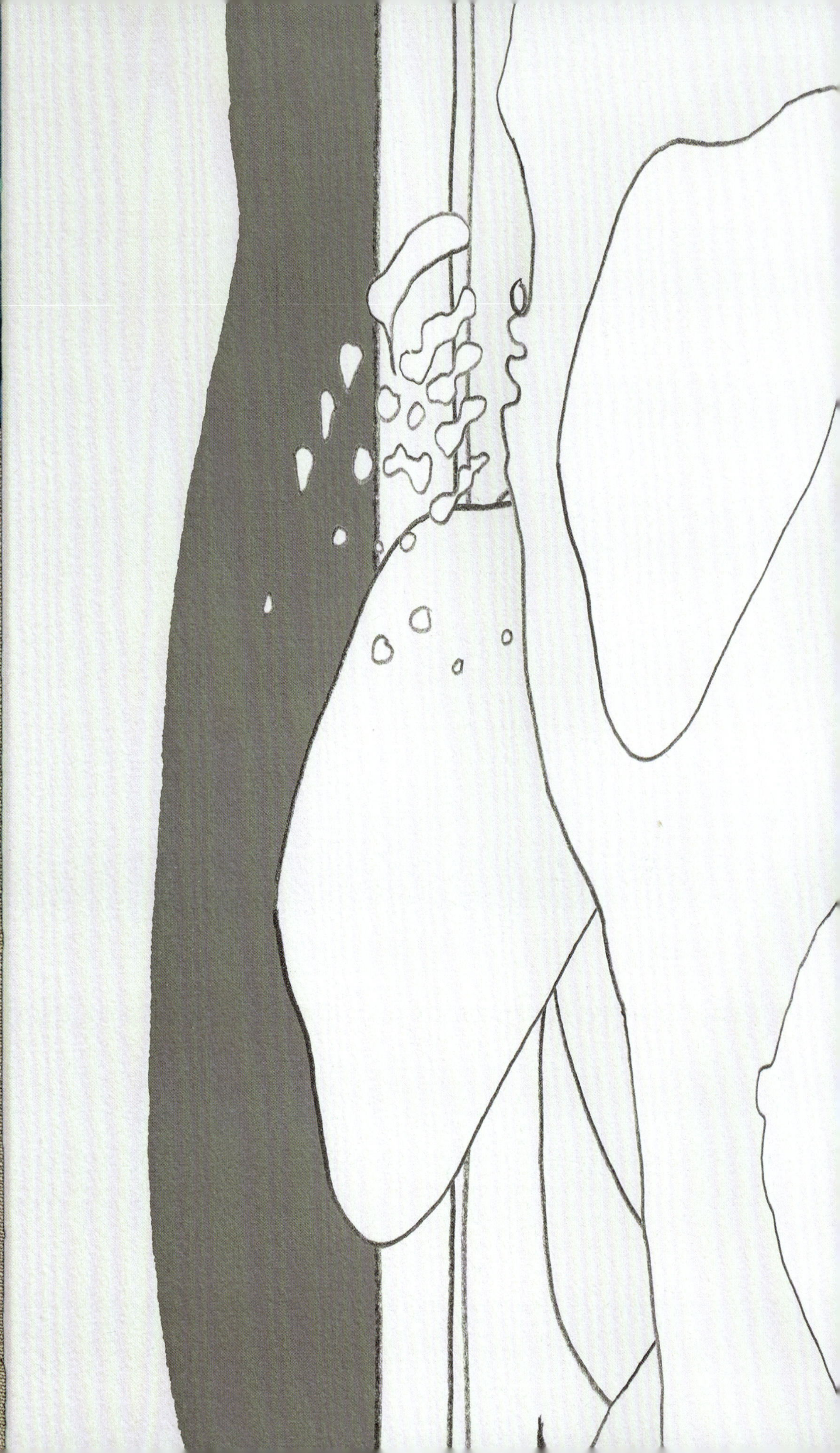

Spontex 009 / Feeling again | 2019

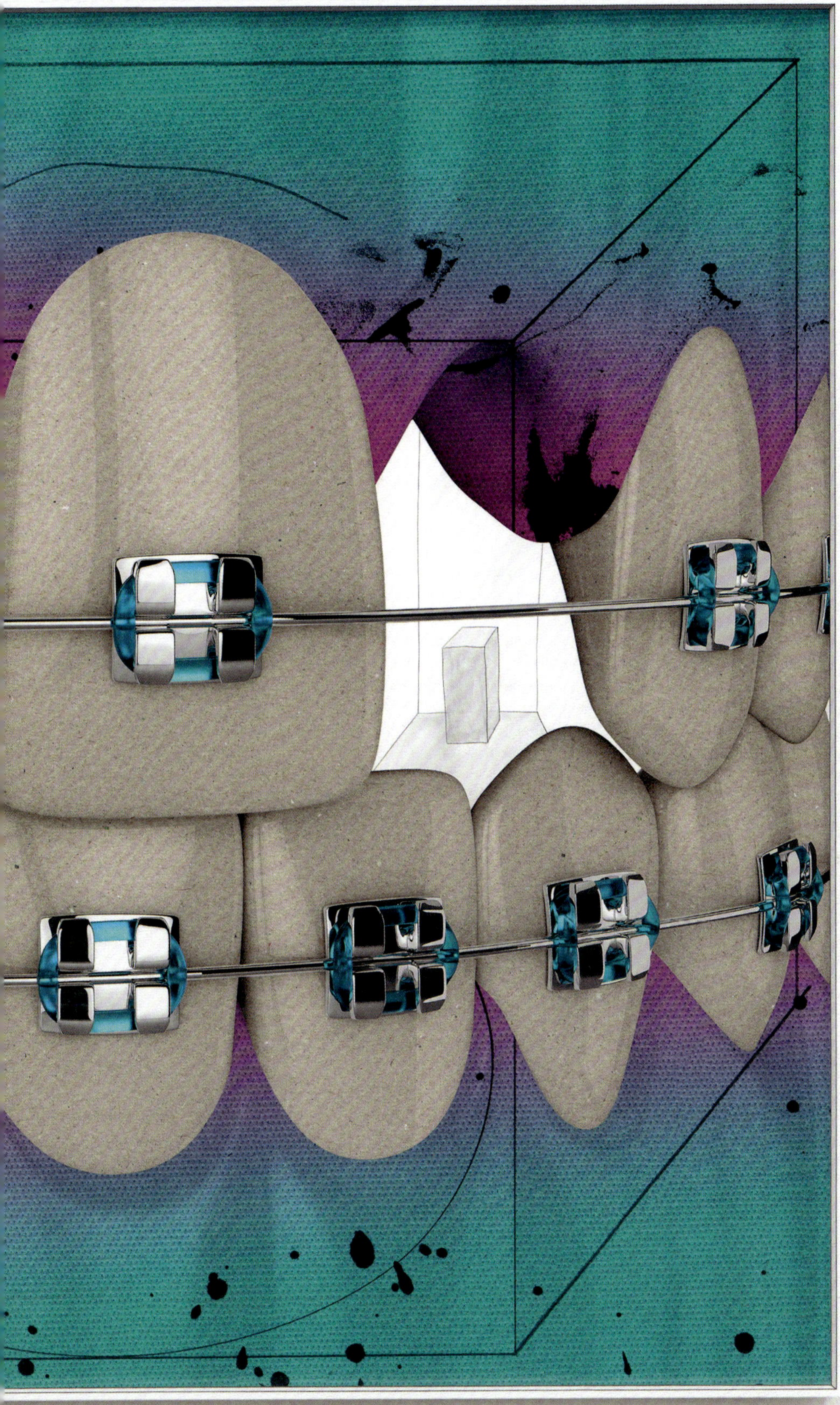

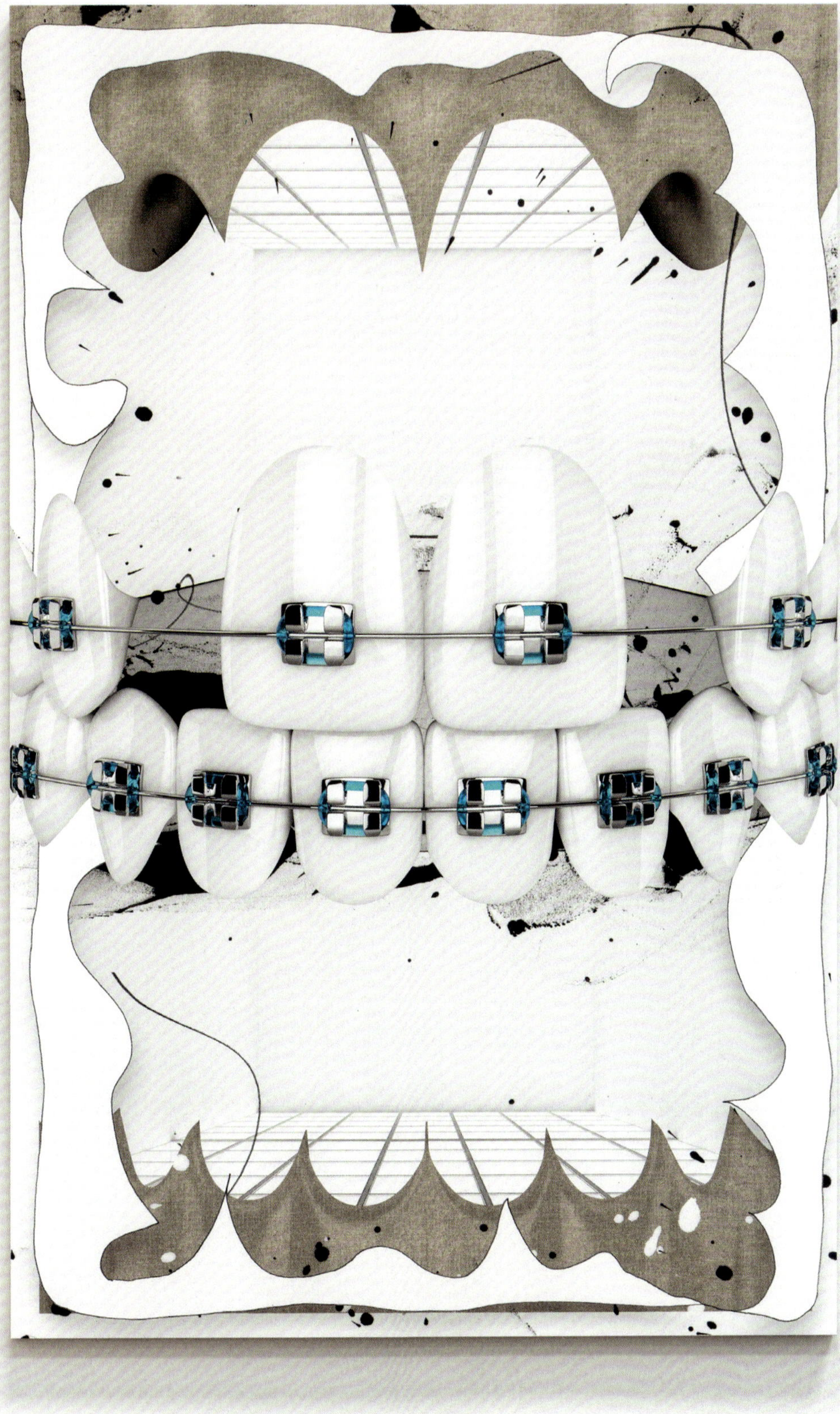

Untitled (Teeth1) I 2019

Untitled (Spikes) | 2019

Untitled (The Show) I 2019

The Pest / Der Schädling I 2019

The hand that feeds I 2019

Untitled (exhibition space) | 2019

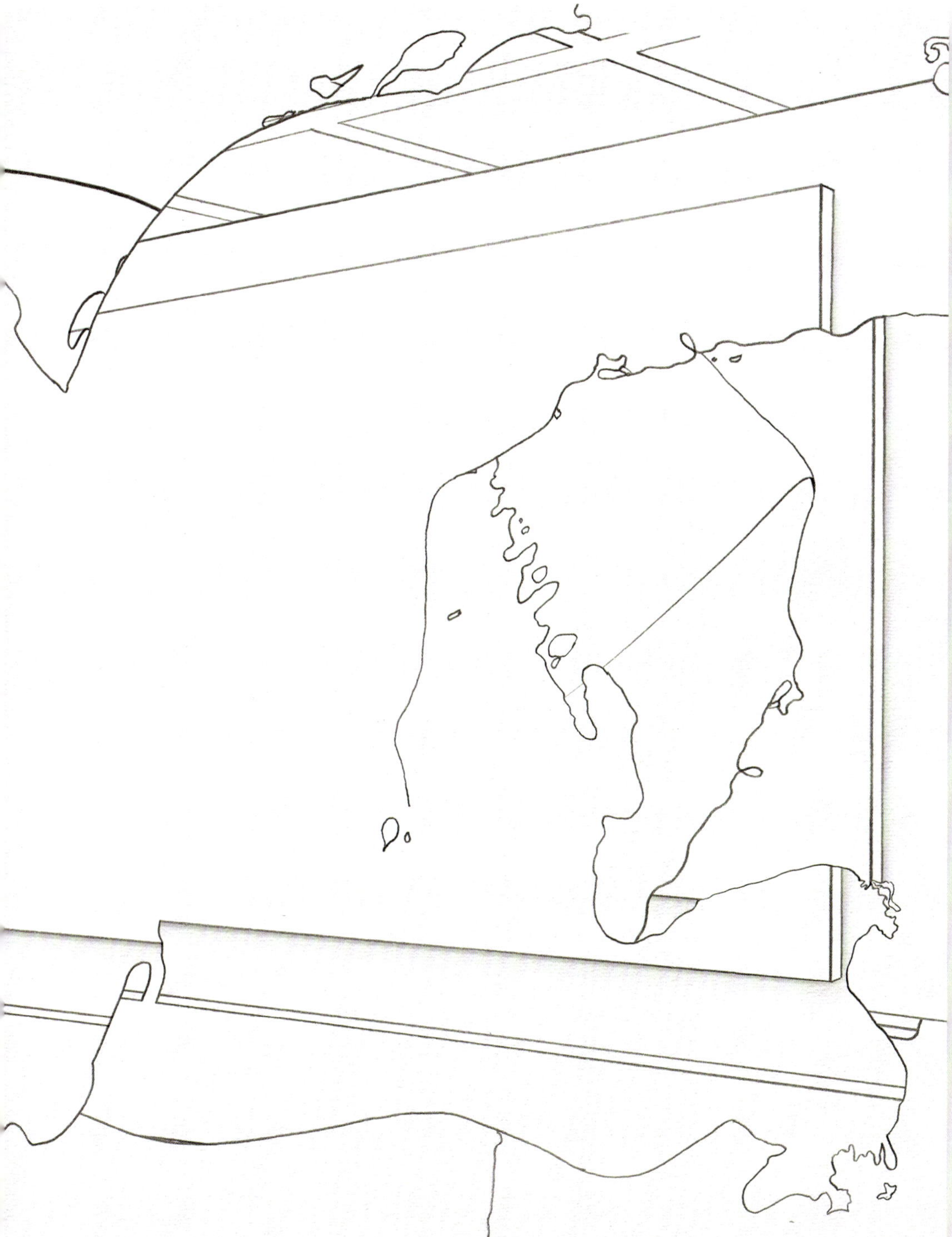

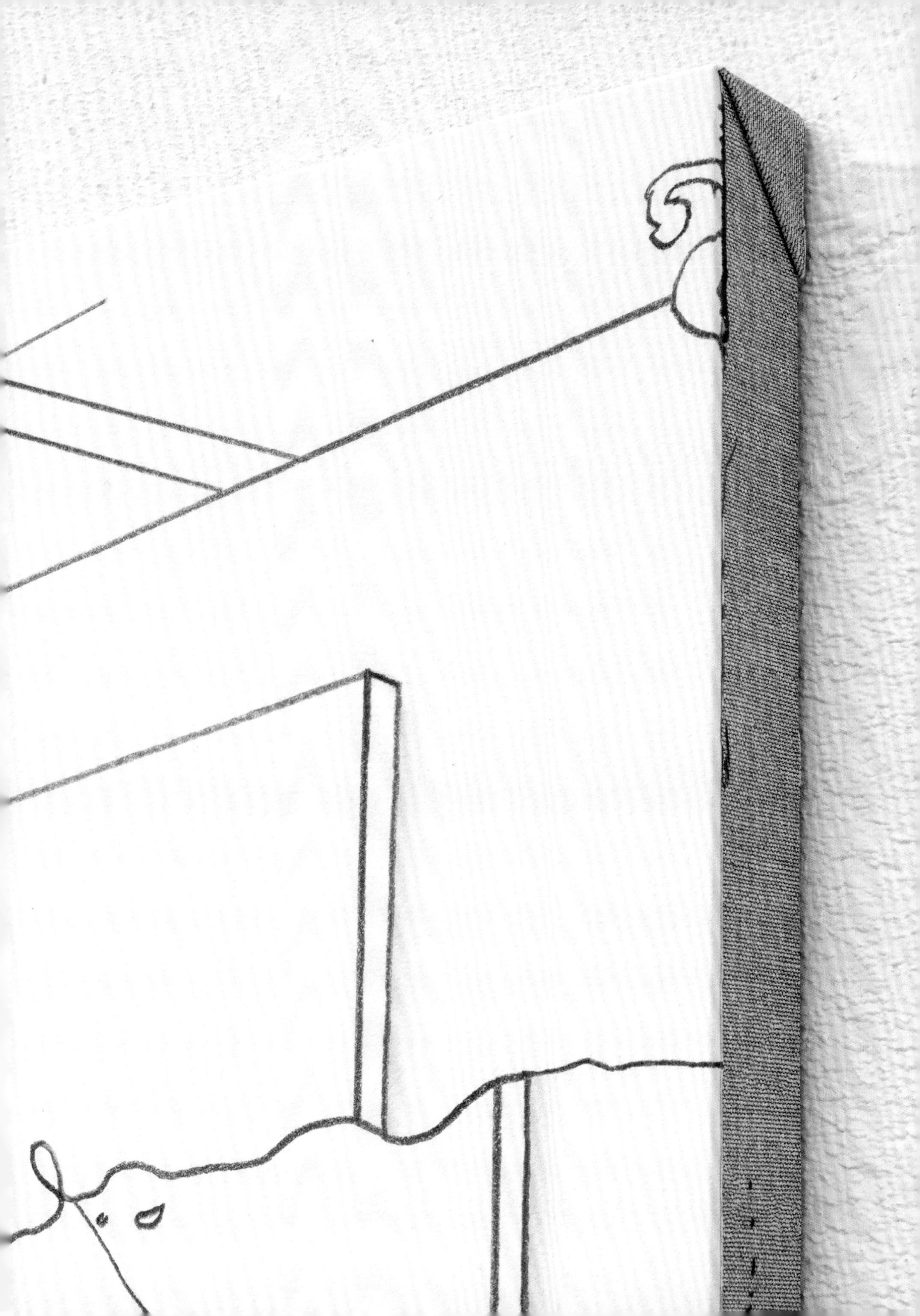

OT0053-B
Male diese Karte aus
und höre auf dein Herz
B

Spontex
Entdecken Sie jetzt unsere
Handschuhe im neuen Design
Hausputz
Wash-Ups
Feeling
Comfort Deluxe
Wussten Sie, dass Malen
zur Entspannung beiträgt?
Sammeln Sie die 5 verschiedenen
Motive und malen Sie sie aus!
Teilen Sie die farbigen Karten in Ihren sozialen
Netzwerken mit #spontexmandala. Wir werden
die Besten auf Facebook veröffentlichen.

#SpontexMandala

Spontex_007 I 2019

#SpontexMandala | Natalia Hug Gallery | 2019

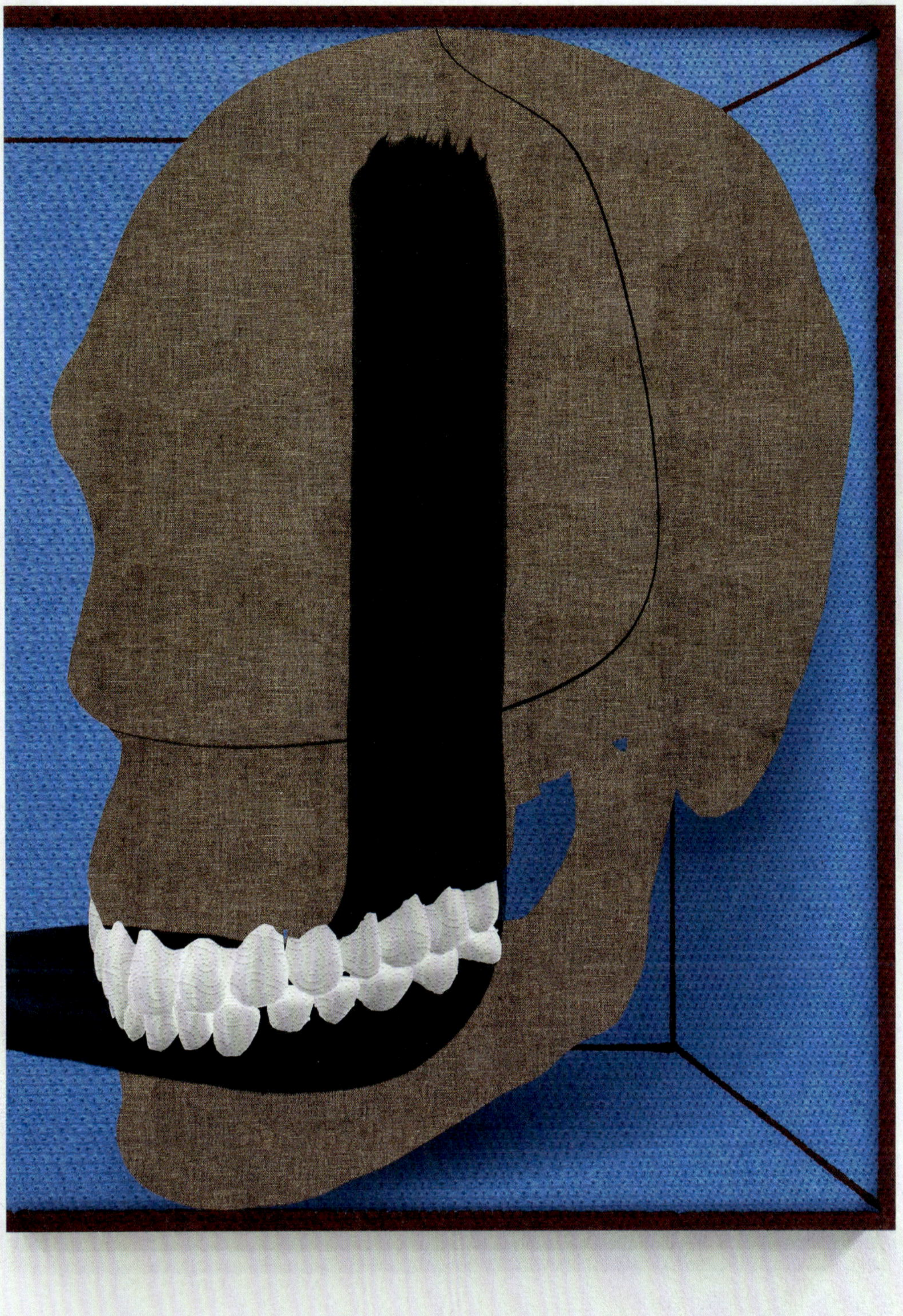

Spontex_005 | 2019

Next Generations | Museum Morsbroich, Leverkusen | 2018

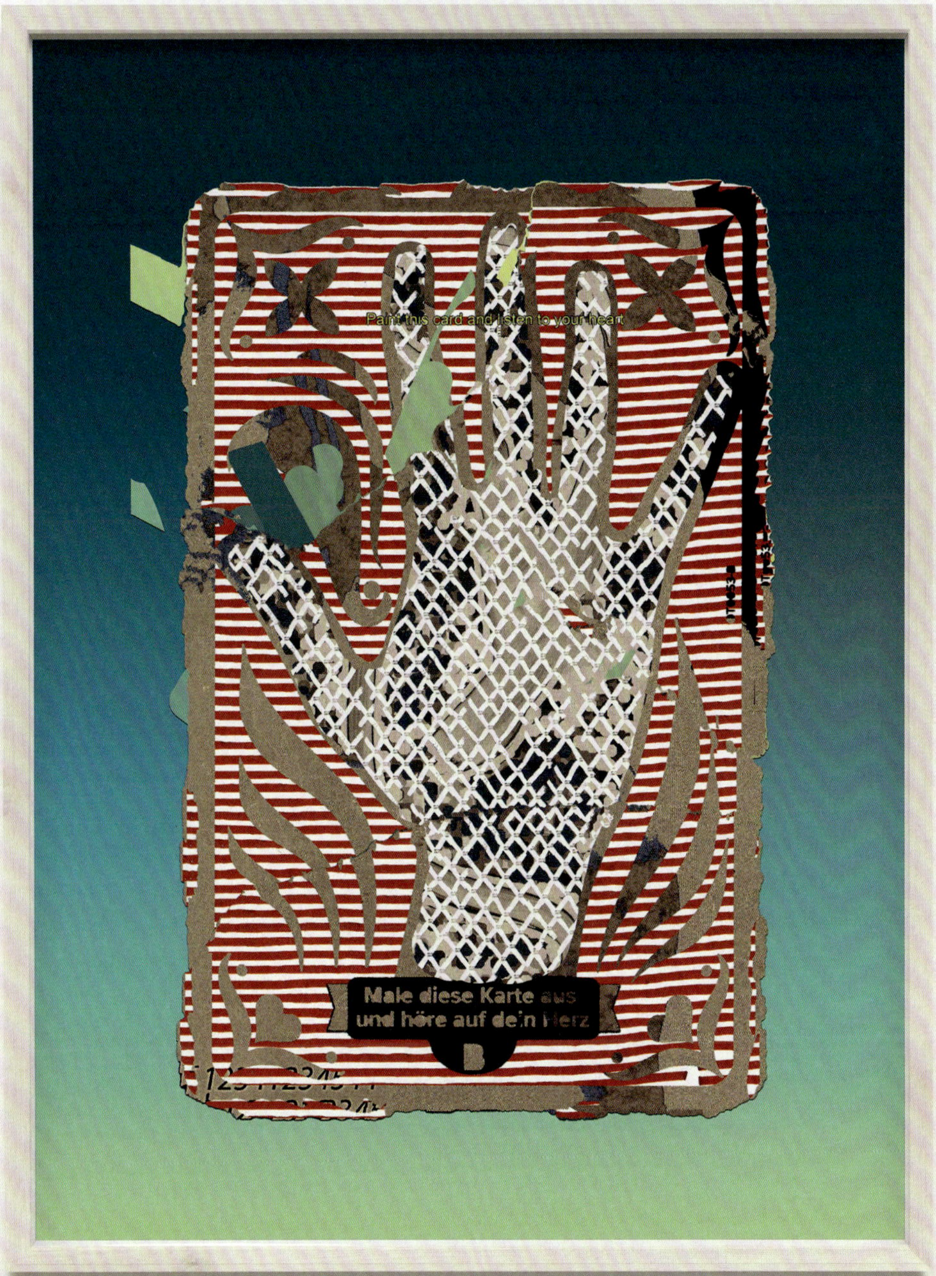

#SpontexMandala (Listen to your Heart) | 2018

#SpontexMandala_HEART_001 | 2018

#SpontexMandala_SMILE_001 | 2018

#SpontexMandala_HEART_001 | 2018

Spontex_002 | 2018

Spontex_003 | 2018

Malerische Freuden.

Ein Gespräch zwischen Johannes Bendzulla und Moritz Scheper

Oktober 2020

MS: Um unserem Gespräch ein bisschen Drive zu geben, habe ich mir ein paar teilweise überspitzte Thesen zurechtgelegt, mit denen ich dich konfrontieren möchte. Die erste davon lautet wie folgt: Auch wenn sich wahrscheinlich niemand jemals selber so bezeichnet hat – du bist ein *Post-Internet-Artist!*

JB: Ich fürchte, das stimmt auf eine gewisse Art. Ich bin auf jeden Fall mit diesem Diskurs in Berührung gekommen, als das damals losging, und es hat mich total fasziniert, muss ich sagen. Weil da plötzlich eine krasse Zeitgenossenschaft war, die so aufgeploppt ist, auch in einer Ästhetik, mit der ich selber zu tun hatte. Ich habe meine ganze Jugend über sehr viel Computerspiele gespielt, ich habe also schon lange eine gewisse Affinität zu computergenerierten Bildern. Deswegen fand ich P.I.A. total faszinierend und habe mich damit auch ziemlich viel beschäftigt, auf eine wirklich fast rein formal-ästhetische Art. Also ja, auf eine gewisse Art hat Post-Internet mich beeinflusst. Aber eher in einer Art von komisch affirmativem Flash für so ungefähr zwei Jahre.

MS: Gab es bestimmte Phänomene oder Schlüsselwerke bei *Post-Internet*, die dich fasziniert haben?

JB: Ich habe 2013 diese Ausstellung „Speculations on Anonymous Materials" im Fridericianum gesehen, wo das so musealisiert wurde. Und da hat mich schon diese Formensprache begeistert. Diese Art, ich sage mal, mit Materialität, Körperlichkeit und digitaler Abstraktion umzugehen. Das fand ich irgendwie geil, aber das hat dann auch relativ schnell wieder nachgelassen. Ich glaube, das war tatsächlich der Reiz des Neuen, auf so einer ganz einfachen Begeisterungsebene. Ich habe mich dann auch selber ein bisschen verrannt in ein paar ästhetischen Experimenten in der Zeit (lacht). Das wurde aber im künstlerischen Prozess irgendwann langweilig für mich, ich bin da auch kaum zu guten Ergebnissen gekommen.

MS: Ich reite so stark auf Post-Internet herum, weil es bei dir auch so eine gewisse Technophilie gibt, die du vielleicht aus der Zeit noch rübergerettet hast?

Painterly Delights.

A conversation between Johannes Bendzulla and Moritz Scheper

October 2020

MS: To give our conversation here a little momentum, I've come up with a few occasionally hyperbolic theses I'd like to confront you with. The first of them is: even if it's likely no one has ever labelled themselves as such, you're a *post-internet artist!*

JB: I'm worried that's kind of true. This is definitely a discourse I came into contact with when it all kicked off, and I was super fascinated by it, I've got to admit. Because it was crazy how suddenly everyone was sharing in this zeitgeist that just popped up, and it was an aesthetic I also had something to do with myself. I played video games a lot as a teenager, so I've had a kind of affinity with computer-generated images for a long time. That's why I found P.I.A. totally engrossing and engaged with it quite a bit, in a way that was really almost purely formal and aesthetic. So yes, post-internet art has influenced me in some way. But pretty much in a kind of weirdly affirmative flash that lasted about two years.

MS: Were there any particular phenomena or key post-internet works that you were especially into?

JB: I saw the exhibition "Speculations on Anonymous Materials" at the Fridericianum in 2013, when everything was "museified," so to speak. And that formal language excited me even back then. That way of dealing with, I'd say, materiality, corporeality, and digital abstraction. I thought it was cool somehow, but it all wore off again pretty quickly. I think in truth it was the thrill of the new, on a really straightforward buzz level. I got a bit lost in a few aesthetic experiments myself back then, too (laughs). The artistic process just became kind of boring for me though, as I hardly ever ended up with anything good.

MS: I'm going in kind of hard on post-internet because there's also a kind of technophilia about you too, maybe one that you've preserved from back then?

JB: Yes, for sure. I think that one constant in my work are those aesthetic strategies where it's about corporeality, coincidence, the organic, the unpredictable, and the clearly separated—always in contrast to anything you could call "mathematical abstraction." The world we live in is very much defined by binary structures. Like ones and

JB: Ja, auf jeden Fall. Ich glaube, eine Konstante in meiner Arbeit sind ästhetische Strategien, wo es so um Körperlichkeit, Zufall, Organik, das Unvorhersehbare und das klar voneinander Getrennte geht – immer im Kontrast zu etwas, das man „mathematische Abstraktion" nennen könnte. Die Welt, in der wir leben, ist sehr stark von binären Grundstrukturen geprägt. Also beispielsweise 1 und 0 als Basiseinheit für Computeroperationen. Das ist so eine Art konstitutives Grundprinzip, welches unsere ganze Lebenswelt durchwirkt, und das auch extrem reduktionistisch ist. Welches aber völlig selbstverständlich funktioniert und akzeptiert wird. Im Prinzip ist das ganze westliche Denken und die damit einhergehende Weltorganisation noch immer stark von Dualismen geprägt, was mir in vielerlei Hinsicht problematisch vorkommt. „Natur und Kultur", „Realität und Simulation" – das sind solche Gegensatzpaare, auf die sich viele meiner Arbeiten beziehen. Mir geht es immer auch darum, das zu reflektieren. Ich arbeite sehr viel mit Computerästhetik, aber immer so, dass alles so ein bisschen komisch aussieht, in der Simulation nicht ganz realistisch. Entweder zu perfekt oder eben mangelhaft in der technischen Umsetzung. Meist sind das organische Elemente wie Pflanzen, Tiere und menschliche Körperteile. Computerästhetik hat einen Hang zur Asepsis, zu unnatürlicher Perfektion, zum Un- oder Übermenschlichen. Das fasziniert mich schon sehr.

MS: Dann kommt hier die These zu deinem Arbeitsprozess. Und zwar: Deine Arbeit speist sich aus der tiefen Kränkung, kein Maler zu sein.

JB: (lacht) Also ich muss gestehen, dass ich verstehe, warum man mich sowas fragen könnte. Aber ich würde nicht sagen, dass das eine Kränkung ist, nicht so direkt. Weil, ich fühle mich jetzt nicht gekränkt. Ich bin ein großer Freund der Malerei! Das, was ich mir eigentlich am liebsten anschaue an Kunst, ist tatsächlich Malerei. Da gibt es ganz viele ästhetische Strategien, bei denen man aus Material – aus abstraktem Material, reiner Farbe – eben Dinge schafft, die auf die erkennbare Welt rekurrieren, bei denen aber gleichzeitig das Material immer als Material präsent bleibt. Also es tritt nie zurück, wie zum Beispiel bei einem fotografischen oder digitalen Bild, bei dem die Materialität total in den Hintergrund tritt. Dieser innere Widerstand zwischen dem Dargestellten und den Materialien der Darstellung, das ist für mich ein ganz elementarer Widerspruch, den ich in der Kunst total wichtig finde. Auch die Tatsache, dass die Handlungen der malenden Person materielle Spuren hinterlassen, anhand derer man als BetrachterIn Entscheidungen und Prozesse nachvollziehen kann, finde ich extrem spannend. Malerische Handlungen sind keine symbolischen Gesten, sondern manifestieren sich ganz konkret, eben materiell, und haben deshalb eine ganz besondere Kraft für mich. Der Grundanspruch meiner Arbeit ist, im/in der BetrachterIn so eine Art von konstruktiver Entfremdung von der Welt hervorzurufen, die die Dinge und ihr Verhältnis zueinander vielleicht erschüttert und dank der sie neu gedacht werden können. Ich benutze zwar gerne affirmative Grundelemente, um Leute zum Einstieg zu bewegen, aber fundamental geht es auch immer um so eine Art von Entfremdungsmoment. Und dieses Entfremdungsmoment erzeugt man eben auch dadurch, dass man die eigenen Mittel der Darstellung so ein bisschen „zur Aufführung" bringt und die Dinge dabei nicht eins zu eins ineinander übergehen. Und das ist auf jeden Fall eine malerische Qualität, die ich immer auch in meine tatsächlich zum großen Teil digitale Arbeit mit einzubauen versuche.

MS: Lass uns doch mal zwei dieser Techniken, die immer wieder bei dir auftauchen, genauer anschauen, vielleicht kannst du ein bisschen was dazu sagen, wie du die einsetzt. Zum einen Trompe-l'œils und daran anschließend, oder sich daran reibend, Glitches. Du mobilisierst sie auf eine gewisse Art und Weise, die sich ständig wiederholt. Man hat den Eindruck (lacht), du möchtest was damit bezwecken …

JB: Ja, absolut. Ich denke, der Zufall ist total wichtig, auch als quasi gegenmathematisches Moment. So würde ich das einfach mal nennen. Dass man in der digitalen Sphäre versucht, mit dem Zufall zu arbeiten, Situationen zu schaffen, in denen der eigene Plan nicht aufgeht und so auch Unerwartetes entstehen kann, das ist auf jeden Fall total wichtig für mich. Im Digitalen immer auch Fehlerpotentiale mit einzubauen.

(Weiter auf Seite 119)

zeros as the basic units of computer operations. This is in a way a basic constitutive principle that permeates the entire world we live in, and which is also extremely reductionist. But it works and is accepted as totally natural. In principle, dualisms are very strongly present in the entirety of Western thought and the way of organizing the world that goes with it, and this is something that to me seems problematic in very many ways. Nature/culture, reality/simulation—these are the kinds of oppositions a lot of my work refers to. For me, the point is always to reflect on this. I work with computer aesthetics a lot, but in a way that makes everything look a little weird, a not-quite-realistic simulation. Either too perfect, or put together with technical faults. Usually with organic elements like plants, animals, and human body parts. Computer aesthetics tend towards asepsis, an unnatural perfection, to being inhuman or superhuman. And this is something that really intrigues me.

MS: Next, a thesis on the methods in your work. And it's this: that your work feeds off of the deep humiliation of not being a painter.

JB: (laughs) Well, I've got to admit I can understand why you'd ask me something like that. But I wouldn't say it's a humiliation, nothing as direct as that. I mean, I don't feel humiliated right now. I'm a big fan of painting! Painting is actually the thing that I really like looking at, in terms of art. There are all kinds of aesthetic strategies where you can take matter—abstract materials, pure color—and create things that recognizably refer back to the world, while the material still always retains a presence as a material. So it never recedes like in a photographic or digital image, where the materiality all but disappears. This internal opposition between what's represented and the materials used for that representation is a really fundamental opposition for me, something that I find super important in art. Even the fact that the actions of the person painting leave material traces behind, which then allow you as a viewer to understand certain decisions and processes, that's something I finds really stimulating. A painter's actions aren't symbolic gestures. They manifest themselves in a very tangible way, in a material way, and that's why I feel they have a very unique power. The basic aspiration of my work is to evoke in the viewer a kind of constructive estrangement from the world, one that might even act to shake things up, including their relationships to each other, and thus offer a basis for rethinking them. So while I do like to use basic affirmative elements to get people on board, it's fundamentally always also about some moment of estrangement. And this moment of estrangement is created by "staging" your own means of representation, so to speak, without the things merging into each other, one-to-one. And that is definitely a painterly quality that I always try to build into my work, which is actually mostly digital.

MS: Let's take a closer look at two of these techniques, which crop up with you time and again. Maybe you can say something about how you use them. Firstly trompe-l'œil, and then also—or maybe by contrast—glitches. You mobilize these in a specific way that is repeated constantly. One gets the impression (laughs) you're trying to achieve something with them...

JB: Yes, definitely. I think chance is super important, even as a kind of counter-mathematical moment. So that's basically how I would label it. In the digital arena you try to work with chance, to create situations where your plan doesn't actually work out and unexpected things are also able to emerge. That's definitely something that's super important to me. Always include the potential for error within the digital.

MS: The definition of "glitch" that I found is "temporary false statement in a logic circuit."

JB: Oh, yeah, that's nice. I'd not come across that. Creating something like that aesthetically, even with digital means, is something I actually kind of like. And as for the second question... exactly, trompe-l'œil. What I find particularly cool about trompe-l'œil is the moment of disillusionment—the illusion and the simultaneous disillusionment. When I work with trompe-l'œil, it's often in an aesthetic framework that's still halfway plausible. That means that in my works there are faked image elements with simulated plasticity that—with regard to spatial depth—are still on a relatively realistic scale. The simulated picture frames that appear in many images, for example. I repeatedly use optical illusions that take place just underneath the surface of the image and thus appear

plausible, so it takes the viewer a relatively long time to register that something's not right. And that's also just a very contemporary aesthetic—after all, we work with screens all the time; with flat displays, that is. Creating an illusion of plasticity also just kind of means, let's say, getting closer to the basic constant of human perception—that spatiality is super important to how we orient ourselves. That's why things like user interfaces are designed to help us navigate, and why a lot of what we get up to on our screens is conceived using that logic. This is a very self-explanatory, aesthetic, and functional moment that we deal with every day. Focusing on this digital-aesthetic moment, demonstrating it in a particular way and constantly playing around with it too, these things are all kind of important to me.

MS: It seems like dysfunctionality is important to you, then. Like, trompe-l'œil with disillusionment, and of course glitches are also a form of non-functioning. Is it key for you to focus on dysfunctionality, to represent it, to produce it, or would that reading of mine be off the mark?

JB: No (laughs), dysfunctionality is cool. Because, well, functionality obviously just means that you have a particular idea of how things should go. And within the parameters of what is good/bad or what works/doesn't work, certain goals are or aren't met. And for me that's also the potential of art, in a totally old-school way—that it dissolves these kinds of categorizations a little. Functionality in and of itself is often only seemingly evident. Because there are... things which everyone seems to agree on because they are pragmatically functional and so they generate something positive. Things for which it seems totally plausible to a lot of people that they are positive.

MS: But which at the same time exclude other things, and so marginalize them.

JB: Exactly, yeah. Definitely.

MS: I want to come back to my thesis on why painting is so important. Your approach obviously goes beyond a pure interest in aesthetic strategies. In your work, does painting also function as a kind of cipher for art in general?

JB: It actually does, sometimes. Or for a particular idea of art, at least, one that has to do with expressivity, the performance of individuality, and uninterrupted subjectivity. For me, ideas of immediacy also play a role in this. Other [German] buzzwords crop up a lot in this context, like intrinsic motivation, ability to innovate, creativity, and the lone warrior. More than anything, I'm interested in popular images of artists and their reception in other social spheres, and here the figure of the painter is still unrivalled. In my art practice and my organization, I repeatedly encounter what I see as highly problematic issues that understandably play hardly any role in the popular reception of artistic creativity and subjectivity.

MS: You mean problematic in that imperatives to subjectification emerge and then, for example, personal self-actualization comes to play a central role in the sphere of work alongside waged work as a source of income?

JB: Yes. There are definitely tendencies towards a certain self-exploitation, and these are also related to this kind of idea of subjectivity. Like, the idea that the work that you perform, waged work, is also supposed to be super meaningful on a personal, spiritual, and self-fulfillment level. We live in a society in which gainful employment does not even necessarily just have a life-sustaining function; it also has a deeper one, which in many ways is really amazing. But this also leads to problems. To moments when boundaries dissolve in a certain way; or to work no longer being adequately paid, or being paid via a kind of symbolic capital with a value for the worker that is often uncertain and volatile. The disappearance of solidarity is another issue, a result of the lone-warrior spirit I just mentioned. I definitely see a connection between these phenomena and the idea of art or the artist-subject as understood in a popular sense—and not just in the fully nuanced, academic sense, where there has obviously been a highly diverse range of thinking for decades now. But I've also come across many straight-up problematic things through very personal experiences, through my own artistic work and reflecting on my own positions.

MS: What things specifically? Something like the artist as the inaugurator of liberalization of the labor economy, for example?

JB: That would be one example. If you want to motivate people to work at a high level, then the best thing is to mobilize them as complete, complex personalities. And when people aren't motivated by "external" incentives

MS: Die Definition, die ich für einen „Glitch“ gefunden habe, lautet: „eine temporäre Falschaussage in logischen Schaltungen“.

JB: Ah ja, das ist schön. Die kannte ich noch nicht. Ja, aber genau sowas ästhetisch zu erzeugen, auch mit digitalen Mitteln, finde ich irgendwie gut. Und die zweite Frage ... genau: Trompe-l'œils. Was ich bei Trompe-l'œils ganz toll finde, ist das Moment der Ent-Täuschung. Also die Täuschung und die gleichzeitige Ent-Täuschung. Wenn ich mit Trompe-l'œils arbeite, dann sehr häufig in einem ästhetischen Rahmen, der noch halbwegs plausibel ist. Das heißt, es gibt in meinen Arbeiten gefakte Bildelemente mit vorgetäuschter Plastizität, welche – was die Raumtiefe angeht – immer noch einem verhältnismäßig realistischen Maßstab entsprechen. Die simulierten Bilderrahmen in vielen Bildern sind so ein Beispiel. Ich verwende immer wieder optische Täuschungen, die sich knapp unterhalb der Bildoberfläche abspielen und die deshalb den BetrachterInnen relativ lang plausibel erscheinen. Das ist einfach auch eine ganz zeitgenössische Ästhetik, schließlich arbeiten wir die ganze Zeit mit Screens, also quasi mit Anzeigen, die flach sind. Das Vortäuschen von Plastizität ist einfach auch eine Art von, sagen wir mal, Zugehen auf die Grundkonstante menschlicher Wahrnehmung, dass Räumlichkeit für uns total wichtig ist, um uns zu orientieren. Und deswegen sind zum Beispiel Benutzeroberflächen und ganz vieles von dem, was wir auf Screens veranstalten, jener Logik entsprechend konzipiert, um uns die Navigation zu erleichtern. Das ist ein ganz selbstverständliches, ästhetisches und funktionales Moment, mit dem wir täglich zu tun haben. Dieses digital-ästhetische Moment zu thematisieren, es auf eine gewisse Art vorzuführen und auch immer wieder damit rumzuspielen, ist mir irgendwie wichtig.

MS: Offenbar ist Dysfunktionalität dir dann wichtig. Also Trompe-l'œils mit der Enttäuschung und Glitches eben auch mit einer Form des Nicht-Funktionierens. Spielt es für dich eine zentrale Rolle, Dysfunktionalität zu thematisieren, darzustellen, zu produzieren, oder geht meine Lesart da ins Leere?

JB: Nein (lacht), Dysfunktionalität ist ganz toll. Weil, naja, Funktionalität bedeutet ja einfach nur, dass man eine bestimmte Vorstellung davon hat, wie Dinge zu laufen haben. Und innerhalb der Parameter, was gut/schlecht oder funktional/nicht funktional ist, werden dann eben bestimmte Zwecke erfüllt oder eben nicht. Und das ist für mich auch, ganz oldschool, ein Potential von Kunst, dass man solche Kategorisierungen ein bisschen auflöst. Gerade Funktionalität hat ja häufig so eine Scheinevidenz. Denn es gibt (Pause) so Dinge, auf die sich scheinbar alle einigen können, weil sie in einem pragmatischen Sinne funktional sind und dadurch etwas Positives erzeugen; bei denen es sehr vielen Leuten also total plausibel erscheint, dass sie positiv sind.

MS: Was gleichzeitig aber Anderes ausschließt, ausgrenzt.

JB: Ja genau. Auf jeden Fall.

MS: Ich wollte nochmal zurückkommen auf meine These bezüglich der Frage, warum die Malerei so wichtig ist. Dein Ansatz geht ja offenbar über so ein reines Interesse für ästhetische Strategien hinaus. Funktioniert Malerei in deiner Arbeit auch so ein bisschen als Chiffre für die Kunst im Allgemeinen?

JB: Ja, manchmal schon. Oder zumindest für eine bestimmte Auffassung von Kunst, die mit Expressivität, performter Individualität und ungebrochener Subjektivität zu tun hat. Auch Vorstellungen von Unmittelbarkeit spielen hier eine Rolle für mich. Weitere häufig in diesem Zusammenhang genannte Schlagworte sind ja Intrinsische Motivation, Innovationskraft, Kreativität und Einzelkämpfertum. Mich interessieren vor allem populäre Bilder von Künstlertum und deren Rezeption in anderen gesellschaftlichen Feldern, und da ist die Figur der Malerin bzw. des Malers immer noch ungeschlagen. In meiner eigenen künstlerischen Praxis und Selbstorganisation sind mir immer wieder – aus meiner Sicht – hochproblematische Aspekte begegnet, die in der populären Rezeption von künstlerischer Kreativität und Subjektivität verständlicherweise kaum eine Rolle spielen.

MS: Du meinst, das ist insofern problematisch, als dann Subjektivitierungsimperative aufkommen und z. B. in der Arbeitswelt neben der Lohnarbeit als Einkommensquelle auch noch die persönliche Selbstverwirklichung eine zentrale Rolle spielt?

JB: Ja. Es gibt auf jeden Fall gewisse Selbstausbeutungstendenzen, die mit so einer Vorstel-

lung von Subjektivität auch zu tun haben. Also die Vorstellung davon, dass die Arbeit, die man leistet, Lohnarbeit, dass die auch gleichzeitig auf einer persönlichen, spirituellen, selbsterfüllenden Ebene unheimlich viel Sinn machen sollte. Wir leben in einer Gesellschaft, in der auch Erwerbsarbeit nicht notwendigerweise einfach nur eine lebenserhaltende, sondern auch eine tiefergehende Funktion hat, was ja in vielerlei Hinsicht total schön ist. Das führt aber eben auch zu Problemen. Zum Beispiel zu gewissen Entgrenzungsmomenten; oder dass die Arbeit nicht mehr ausreichend finanziell abgegolten wird, sondern auch durch so eine Art von symbolischem Kapital, dessen Wert für die arbeitende Person häufig unsicher, volatil ist. Entsolidarisierung ist ein weiterer Aspekt, hervorgerufen durch den eben genannten Einzelkämpferspirit. Ich sehe da auf jeden Fall einen Zusammenhang zwischen diesen Umständen und der Vorstellung von Kunst oder vom KünstlerInnensubjekt, wie es in einem populären Sinne entworfen wird – nicht nur in einem ganz ausdifferenzierten, akademischen Sinne, denn da gibt es natürlich schon seit x Jahrzehnten die unterschiedlichsten Entwürfe. Auch durch ganz persönliche Erlebnisse, durch meine eigene künstlerische Arbeit und das Reflektieren der eigenen Position sind mir da viele einfach auch problematische Aspekte begegnet.

MS: Welche ganz konkret? So etwas wie der/die KünstlerIn als StichwortgeberIn für eine Liberalisierung der Arbeitsökonomie zum Beispiel?

JB: Zum Beispiel. Wenn man Leute dazu motivieren möchte, hohe Leistungen zu erbringen, funktioniert das am besten, wenn man versucht, sie als gesamte komplexe Persönlichkeit zu mobilisieren. Und, dass die Leute nicht mehr durch „äußere“ Anreize motiviert werden, durch die Anhäufung von Geld und Status beispielsweise, sondern dass sie Aufgaben gerne und auch deshalb mit voller Energie übernehmen, weil sie von deren Wichtigkeit überzeugt sind. Um dann eben das gesamte Potential dieser Leute abzurufen und auch eben zu kapitalisieren, im Sinne von finanziellem Kapital.

MS: Jetzt sind wir schon mittendrin in dem, was meine dritte These werden sollte: Du brauchst die Erwerbsarbeit für die künstlerische Arbeit. Also das meint einerseits vielleicht, dass du in deiner Arbeit so eine soziologische Betrachtung der Verhedderungen von Kreativität, Kreativwirtschaften, Arbeitsökonomien leistest. Aber deine eigene Erwerbsarbeit informiert deine künstlerische Arbeit ja auch, würde ich sagen. Vielleicht insofern, als du über die Eingebundenheit in ökonomische Prozesse außerhalb deiner künstlerischen Arbeit dann vielleicht auch dieses Ideal des/der sich selbst verwirklichenden Künstlers/Künstlerin hinterfragst, und, inwiefern dieses Bild in eine neoliberale Verwertungslogik übersetzt worden ist, um Motivationsprozesse in Gang zu setzen. Ich kann mir vorstellen, dass das vielleicht über deine eigene Arbeitserfahrung entstanden ist.

JB: Eigentlich nicht, das kam eher über soziologische Literatur in Gang. Ich habe eben während des Studiums gemerkt, dass viele Anforderungen – berufliche, künstlerische und private – sich auf ganz komische Arten und Weisen, auch zwischenmenschlich, in diesem Kunstberuf verschränken. Und ich habe gemerkt, dass das bereits anfing, leichte Dissonanzen zu erzeugen. Durch einen reinen Zufall bin ich in einem Seminar von Juliane Rebentisch gelandet, die damals auch total auf diesem Thema war. Ich bin eigentlich ein sehr politischer Mensch. Also, ich interessiere mich extrem für Politik und lese regelmäßig ziemlich viel darüber. Das hat aber bis zu dem Zeitpunkt in meiner künstlerischen Arbeit nie eine Rolle gespielt und ich habe mich dann irgendwann im Studium gefragt: Ist das normal (lacht) oder ist das nicht irgendwie auch merkwürdig? Und dann gab es da diesen Moment, als eine Art Meta-Politisierung meiner eigenen künstlerischen Rolle stattgefunden hat. Also, dass ich mich selbst und meine Arbeit plötzlich in einem größeren gesellschaftlichen Kontext reflektiert habe und dass diese ganze soziologische Betrachtung der eigenen Existenz und der eigenen Arbeit plötzlich total wichtig wurde.

MS: Wenn man deine beiden Tätigkeiten nebeneinanderstellt, also zum einen die Arbeit, die du für den Pressespiegel machst, für den du Diskurse bündelst, stauchst und konsumierbar präsentierst als Erwerbsarbeit, und zum anderen die Kunst: Ließe sich dann sagen, dass die Lohnarbeit deine künstleri-

anymore—by accumulating money and status, for example—they take on their responsibilities with full energy, because they really feel those responsibilities to be important. And this can lead to the entire potential of those people being tapped into—to them being capitalized on, in the sense of financial capital.

MS: We're already in the thick of what was going to be my third thesis: that you need gainful employment for your artistic work. So on the one hand this means that in your work, you take a sociological view of the entanglements of creativity, creative economies, and labor economies. But then your own gainful employment does also inform your artistic work, I'd say. Maybe in as far as you interrogate the embeddedness in economic processes outside your artistic work, and maybe also this ideal of the self-actualizing artist and the extent to which this image has been transposed into a neoliberal logic of value-creation, in order to initiate motivational processes. I can imagine this all as having arisen from your own experiences of work.

JB: It actually didn't, it was more from sociological literature. When I was a student I noticed that many demands—professional, artistic, personal—are entangled in the art profession in a super strange way, and in an interpersonal way too. And I noticed that was already starting to create small dissonances. By total coincidence, I ended up in a Juliane Rebentisch seminar that was really focused on this. I'm actually a very political person, so I'm extremely interested in politics and regularly read a fair amount about it. But that had never played a role in my artistic work, until at some point, as a student, I asked myself if this was normal (laughs), or if it wasn't actually kind of strange. And then there was this moment where a kind of meta-politicization of my own role occurred, when I suddenly reflected on myself and my work within its wider social context. This entire sociological reflection on my own existence and work suddenly became super important.

MS: If you compare your two jobs, one where you're employed doing press reviews, bundling, compressing, and presenting discourse for consumption, and then on the other hand the art, could it then be said that waged work strongly informs your artistic work in that the discursivity in the artistic work doesn't happen in any strongly defined way and instead comes in from the outside?

JB: That's maybe almost a kind of compensatory relationship. I'm super interested in art discourse, or at least in those discourses that are connected to social politics. I'm especially interested in the less specialist and more popular engagement with art/culture and the entire politics that go along with it. The press review is one way for me to get into this and make it productive again. But this isn't something that has to be immediately fed back into my art.

MS: So you see this service you provide, that you read these texts and condense them and present them twice a month as a press review, you see that as being explicitly not a part of your artistic project?

JB: Yes, for sure. I see it more as a service (laughs). There are very pragmatic decisions that I make based on very comprehensible criteria for choosing specific things. I don't really see it as creative, I've got to say. I also don't think it's necessary to see it as somehow especially creative.

MS: And you don't have to, I don't think. But to me it seems to be a key part your practice, which shows an interest in macro-social phenomena. This sort of work obviously isn't typical to the ivory tower. But yours seems instead to be more of a basic interest, which is then presented in a more nuanced way in your performance of a service. That's why I ask whether you make a hard distinction here. But I understand how that could be rejected.

JB: In the works produced recently, there is a lot of material that is almost completely free of any kind of basic interest in sociology or society. All the tooth works, for example. There's really a pure pleasure in particular aesthetics and also in the intention to create a certain kind of uncomfortable feeling. There's actually relatively little reference made back to particular discourses, at least intentionally. Links can be made, obviously: white teeth, the white cube, there are obviously particular social implications. Whether you can read the economic prosperity of a person from their teeth, for example, all these kinds of things. Cleanliness and connected ideas of how

sche Arbeit stark informiert, indem die Diskursivität in der künstlerischen Arbeit gar nicht so stark stattfindet, sondern eher von außen hineinkommt?

JB: Das ist vielleicht fast so eine Art von kompensatorischem Verhältnis. Ich interessiere mich unheimlich für Kunstdiskurse. Also zumindest für die, die gesellschaftspolitisch angebunden sind. Insbesondere interessiert mich die weniger spezialistenhafte, populäre Auseinandersetzung mit Kunst/Kultur und die ganze Politik, die da dranhängt. Der Pressespiegel ist so eine Möglichkeit, mich damit zu beschäftigen und das auch wieder produktiv zu machen. Aber das muss dann halt nicht unbedingt direkt in meine Kunst rein.

MS: Du siehst also diese Dienstleistung, die du machst, dass du diese Texte liest und komprimierst und zweimal monatlich als Pressespiegel präsentierst, das siehst du explizit nicht als Teil deines künstlerischen Projektes an?

JB: Ja, auf jeden Fall. Ich sehe das eher (lacht) als Serviceleistung. Es gibt da ganz pragmatische Entscheidungen, die ich dann treffe, für die es ganz nachvollziehbare Kriterien gibt, warum ich bestimmte Dinge auswähle. Ich sehe das nicht so richtig kreativ, muss ich sagen. Ich finde, es ist auch nicht notwendig, das irgendwie großartig kreativ zu sehen.

MS: Das muss man auch nicht, denke ich. Aber mir scheint das ein grundlegender Aspekt deiner an gesamtgesellschaftlichen Phänomenen interessierten Praxis zu sein. Das ist ja nicht die typische Elfenbeinturm-Arbeit. Sondern es gibt ein Grundinteresse, welches sich dann in deiner Serviceleistung noch ausdifferenziert. Daher die Frage, ob du da den harten Schnitt siehst. Aber ich verstehe, dass man das ausgrenzt.

JB: Bei den Arbeiten, die in letzter Zeit entstanden sind, gibt es ganz viel Material, das fast völlig frei ist von irgendwelchen soziologischen oder gesellschaftlichen Grundinteressen. Die ganzen Zahnarbeiten zum Beispiel. Das ist wirklich die reine Freude an bestimmten Ästhetiken und auch die Absicht, so ein gewisses unangenehmes Gefühl zu erzeugen. Da gibt es wirklich relativ wenig konkrete Bezugnahme auf bestimmte Diskurse – zumindest nicht intentional. Natürlich lassen sich auch da Verbindungen herstellen: weiße Zähne, White Cube, da gibt es natürlich auch gewisse gesellschaftliche Implikationen. Ob man z. B. das ökonomische Wohlergehen einer Person an den Zähnen ablesen kann und lauter solche Sachen. Reinheit und in Zusammenhang damit bestimmte Vorstellungen davon, wie der White Cube als Ausstellungsraum konstituiert ist. Das Ausgrenzen von äußeren Einflüssen und die Idee von Verschmutzungen, das sind so Fragen, die jetzt mit diesen neuen Arbeiten aufkommen. Aber die sind nur relativ locker verbunden mit gesellschaftlichen Diskursen. Das ist gerade eigentlich auch wirklich ein großer Spaß.

MS: Sehr frustrierend, dass du meine vierte These vorweggenommen hast, laut der du mit deiner Arbeit gerade in eine neue Phase eingetreten ist, in der du dein Inventar an Formen und Techniken, die du dir als quasi-rhetorische Instrumente aufgebaut hast, neu kombinierst und zusammensetzt. Da wäre meine Frage gewesen, ob du dich, oder besser gesagt, ob sich deine Kunst aktuell aus ihrer Diskursivität so ein bisschen zurückzieht. Was du ja dann eben genau so beschrieben hast.

JB: Total.

MS: Was aber vielleicht auch stattfindet, stattfinden kann, weil Diskursivität bei dir dann auf dem Standbein (Anm.: die Lohnarbeit) stattfinden kann. Aber lass uns bei diesen neuen Arbeiten bleiben, die du bei Petra Rinck Ende 2020 gezeigt hast. Woher kommt diese Verengung auf das Tafelbild?

JB: Das Tafelbild ist einfach eine tradierte Form der Kunstpräsentation und ich mag es, mich mit Formaten zu beschäftigen, die scheinbar selbstverständlich sind. Und eines der konventionellsten Formate, die ich mir überhaupt vorstellen kann, ist das Bild an der Wand. Das ist auch eine ganz pragmatische Entscheidung gewesen. Weil mir das erlaubt, mit grundlegenden Präsentationsformen herumzuexperimentieren. Da tun sich diverse Möglichkeiten auf, z. B. wie man mit Rahmen umgeht. Das sind auch tatsächlich ganz einfach kunstphilosophische Klassiker, die mich dann interessieren. Dass ein Bild eigentlich zweidimensional wirkt, aber immer auch plastisch ist. Was macht man eigentlich mit dem Rand oder der Seite von einem Bild? Wie geht man damit um? Und was sagt das aus, wie man

Trainee
Trainee

damit umgeht, und so weiter. Da ergeben sich für mich einfach ganz viele Potentiale, mit denen ich gerne arbeite. Es ist ziemlich flach, (lacht) das Bild. Aber es ist eben nicht zweidimensional. Und innerhalb von diesem kleinen plastischen Spielraum, wo quasi Dreidimensionalität eine Rolle spielt, aber eben keine hervorgehobene, vulgäre Rolle hat, wie zum Beispiel in einer Installation oder Plastik oder Skulptur, kann man dann mit solchen Fragen arbeiten. Auf einer relativ subtilen Ebene. Die man quasi so durch die Hintertür einfach immer mitverhandeln kann, ohne dass es so ein Mega-Thema wird. Deswegen mag ich das Tafelbild als das mit konventionellste Medium, das ich mir vorstellen kann.

MS: Ich habe mir dieses komische Buzzwort *painting beside itself* im Zusammenhang mit dir aufgeschrieben. Würdest du da mitgehen oder ist das für dich schon eher *painting painting*? Denn das diskursive Material, welches die Elemente mitschleppen, ist ja jetzt nicht mehr so präsent und die Bilder funktionieren auch ohne einen Anker im Außen.

JB: Hmm, da würde ich wohl eher nicht mitgehen. Ich muss dazu sagen, dass ich mich eine Zeit lang sehr viel mit so Meta-Malerei und den ganzen Klassikern beschäftigt habe. Was ich damals dann tatsächlich am allertollsten fand, ist die Arbeit von Robert Ryman, d. h. eine Art von Malerei, die einfach Grundthemen ihrer eigenen materiellen Bedingungen thematisiert, aber auf eine ganz poetische und spielerische Art und Weise. Also das ist ein Bild, da ist Farbe drauf, dann gibt es eine Signatur, dann muss ein Bild an der Wand befestigt werden. Dass jeder Pinselstrich an sich schon eine Entscheidung beinhaltet und einfach nur diese Entscheidung thematisiert wird, auf so eine gewisse Art. Ich fand das unheimlich minimal, selbstreferentiell und gleichzeitig poetisch. Oder dass zum Beispiel die Farbe Weiß nicht immer die hellste Farbe ist. Sondern dass es dafür bestimmte materielle Voraussetzungen gibt. Wie zum Beispiel: Wir malen auf einem Alu-Träger und dadurch, dass das Licht changiert, ist das Weiß manchmal dunkler als die Reflexion auf dem Metall daneben. Das sind ganz poetische, aber auch total analytische Momente. Diese Kombination fand ich extrem überzeugend, mind-blowing, und das ist eine Art Grundreferenz, wie ich mit ästhetischen Mitteln umgehe. Also spielerisch und analytisch zugleich, ja.

MS: Also du bist Maler, um mal zurück an den Anfang zu gehen.

JB: (lacht) Ich sage mal, ich habe unheimlich viele ästhetische Strategien aus der Malerei übernommen oder zu schätzen gelernt und dann versucht, sie in meine digitale Praxis zu integrieren. Wir haben unheimlich viel mit digitalen Bildern zu tun. Aber das digitale Bild hat ein fundamentales Problem und das ist eben seine Körperlosigkeit, das Verstecken der Mittel der Produktion. Das kennt man vom fotografischen Bild natürlich schon lange. Die Art, wie jetzt digitale Bilder produziert werden, das sind Drucke oder Darstellungen auf einem Monitor, die keine eigene Materialität haben oder eben eine, die einfach nicht mitgedacht wird. Ich finde das ein fundamentales philosophisches Problem in der medialen Vermittlung von Welt. Dieses Thema beschäftigt mich einfach schon seit Ewigkeiten. Unter anderem deshalb bin ich vor knapp zehn Jahren auf Büttenpapier als Bildträger umgestiegen – die raue Oberfläche des Papiers und seine organische Struktur geben den Arbeiten einen „Körper" und erzeugen einen starken taktilen Reiz.

MS: Was sagst du zu dieser Ad-hoc-These: Was du gerade gesagt hast, ist eine gute Zusammenfassung deiner künstlerischen Praxis. Das digitale Bild verschleiert den Herstellungsprozess. Und warum verschleiert es ihn? Weil er teilweise problematisch ist, ausbeuterisch oder selbstausbeuterisch. Und so hängen vielleicht diese beiden Komplexe zusammen, Malerei zum einen, Arbeit von der soziologischen Perspektive aus gesehen auf der anderen Seite. Also, ich denke jetzt nur laut.

JB: Die These ist mir zu steil. (lacht)

MS: Bei den neuen Bildern ist mir eine Wiederholung aufgefallen. Und zwar zeigst du dich darin als komische Figur, was du früher auch schon mal gemacht hast, u. a. als Karl Klammer, dieser nutzlose Assistent von Microsoft. Jetzt wieder als schrumpfköpfiges Monster. Es fällt ja auf, dass du viel mit Selbstportraits arbeitest, aber warum zeigst du dich selber als Hanswurst?

JB: Hmm, gute Frage. Wenn man sich selber als ProtagonistIn irgendwie auch lächerlich macht, finde ich das grundsätzlich eine sympathische

the white cube is constituted as an exhibition space. How to exclude external influences, the idea of contamination—both of these questions crop up in these new works. But their connections to social discourses are fairly loose. And that's something that's actually a lot of fun, too.

MS: It's super frustrating that you took away my fourth thesis, according to which your work has just entered a new phase in which you rephrase and reassemble the inventory of forms and techniques that you have built for yourself as quasi-rhetorical instruments. So my question would have been if you, or rather your art, are currently receding from discursivity a little. Exactly as you described it just now.

JB: Totally.

MS: Maybe this happens, or can happen, when discursivity forms a part of your waged work. But let's stick with these new works that you showed at Petra Rinck in late 2020. What is the origin of this self-imposed restriction to panel paintings?

JB: The panel painting is just a traditional form of art presentation, and I like working with formats that seem like a matter of course. And since a painting on a wall is one of the most conventional formats I can imagine, it was also a very pragmatic decision. Because it makes it possible for me to experiment with basic forms of presentation. So many possibilities are opened up, like how you deal with frames. The fact is that this format is clearly an art-philosophical classic, and it interests me because of that. That the painting seems two-dimensional but is always also sculptural. What do you actually do with the edge or side of a painting? How do you deal with that? And what does the way you deal with it say, and so forth. There are a lot of possibilities that emerge from this for me, and I like working with them. It's fairly flat (laughs), the painting, but it's not just two-dimensional. And within this small, sculptural space of latitude, where three-dimensionality plays a kind of role, but not an elevated, vulgar role like in an installation or statue or sculpture, you can work with these kinds of questions. On a relatively subtle level. You can always negotiate through the back door, so to speak, without it becoming a massive issue. That's why I like the panel painting, as one of the most conventional media I can think of.

MS: I noted down this weird buzz word painting beside itself in connection with you. Would you go along with that or is more a case of painting painting for you? Given that the discursive material that the elements bring along with them isn't present anymore and the paintings function even without an external anchor.

JB: Hmm, I probably wouldn't go along with that. I have to add that for a while I really got involved with meta-painting and all the classics. Back then, the thing I found coolest was Robert Ryman's work, so a kind of painting that focuses on the basic issue of its own material conditions, but in a very poetic and playful manner. So there's a painting, there's paint on it, then there's a signature, then a painting has to be attached to the wall. Every brushstroke in and of itself entails a decision and this very decision is made into a point of focus, and in such a deliberate way. I found it strangely minimal, self-referential, and poetic all at the same time. Or that white isn't always the lightest color, for example, and that there are particular material conditions that determine this. Another example: we paint on an aluminum surface, and when the light changes, the white is sometimes darker than the reflection on the metal beside it. These are very poetic but also totally analytic moments. I found this combination extremely impressive, mind-blowing even, and that's a kind of basic reference as to how I deal with aesthetic resources. So playful and analytic at the same time, yes.

MS: So you are a painter, to go back to where we started.

JB: (laughs) I'd say I've taken an incredible number of aesthetic strategies from painting, or learned to appreciate them, and then tried to integrate them into my digital practice. We spend an amazing amount of time dealing with digital images. But the digital image has a fundamental problem, and that is its very disembodiedness, the hiding of the means of production. This is obviously something long familiar from photographic images. The way digital images are produced now, they're prints or presentations on a monitor with no materiality of their own, or simply a materiality that isn't kept in mind. I think this is a fundamental philosophical problem in

Haltung. Sich als AutorIn nicht so ernst zu nehmen, spiegelt vielleicht so ein bisschen meine Gesamtattitude, weil mir Autorschaft im Sinne von einer persönlichen Hervorbringung von Dingen generell ziemlich suspekt ist. Denn es gibt unglaublich viele Einflüsse, von denen ich mir bewusst bin, dass sie meine Arbeit prägen. Zufälle sind wie gesagt kein Problem für mich, sondern ein produktiver Grundbestandteil meiner Arbeit. Und das reflektiert vielleicht auch ein bisschen mein Auftreten als deren Autor. Ehrlich gesagt habe ich bisher nie darüber nachgedacht, aber es kommt mir irgendwie plausibel vor, dass in dieser Lächerlichkeit der schaffenden Person (lacht) eine große Freiheit steckt. Aber auch so eine gewisse Angreifbarkeit. Ich trete eben nicht autoritär auf. Schließlich ist die eigene Arbeit immer nur eine Behauptung. Das fand ich schon immer mit das Tollste an der Kunst: dass alle immer nur behaupten und es einfach darauf ankommt, wer die geilste, übertriebenste, merkwürdigste, verwegenste und trotzdem plausibelste Behauptung aufstellt und dass genau deshalb Autorität im klassischen Sinne nichts zählt. Das war für mich immer schon ein befreiendes Moment von Kunst. Und so präsentiere ich mich als Autor eben in diversen merkwürdigen, lächerlichen Posen, um meine Position in Frage zu stellen.

MS: ... und das vielleicht auch eingedenk der Offenlegung der problematischen Auswirkungen eines liberalen KünstlerInnenverständnisses, das dann Stichwortgeber wird für die Deregulierung der Arbeitswelt. Ist so eine Form von Lächerlichkeit für dich dann die einzige Möglichkeit, an so etwas wie Kunstmachen festzuhalten?

JB: Sagen wir mal so: ich bin teilnehmender Beobachter in diesem ganzen Zirkus. Dieses Kunstmachen ist in vielerlei Hinsicht problematisch und grotesk, auch durch diese ganzen Verstrickungen, mit denen man da zu tun hat. Mein Grundgefühl ist ein ambivalentes; es gibt sehr viele Dinge, die ich unglaublich sinnvoll und toll finde an der Existenzform, die ich pflege, und es gibt unheimlich viele Aspekte, die ich total bedenklich finde. Das kann ich alles nicht voneinander trennen, da diese positiven und negativen Aspekte für mich alle irgendwie zusammengehören. Ich sage nicht, dass das eine produktive Haltung ist, es ist nur meine ehrliche Haltung. Ich kann mich nicht so richtig auf eine bestimmte Seite stellen in diesem Feld. Und ich glaube oder hoffe, dass meine Arbeiten dieses Involviertsein und auch dieses moralische Dilemma ernst nehmen und nicht versuchen, das aufzulösen oder Ausweichmanöver durchzuführen. Und dass das zu Ergebnissen führen kann, die total problematisch, aber gleichzeitig auch sehr erkenntnisreich sind. Weil sie eben nicht demonstrieren, was man eh schon weiß, sondern Fragen formulieren, die ehrlich sind. In meiner Arbeit schwingt immer ein grundsätzlicher Zweifel daran mit, sich tatsächlich auf eine bestimmte Seite schlagen zu können, aber eben auch die Idee, dass genau das auch eine Qualität sein könnte. Zumindest eine künstlerische oder philosophische Qualität. Ich spreche nicht von einer politischen Qualität oder so. Da gibt es für mich einen klaren Unterschied. Kunst zeigt die Welt wie sie sein *könnte*, und nicht, wie sie sein *sollte*. Das ist meiner Meinung nach ihr spezifisches Potential.

media communication across the world, and it's an issue I've been working with for a long time. That's one of the reasons I switched over to using laid paper as a surface about ten years ago—the roughness of the surface and its organic structure give the works a "body" and a strong tactile appeal.

MS: What would you say to this ad-hoc thesis: what you just said is a good summary of your artistic practice. The digital image obfuscates the production process. And why does it obfuscate it? Because it's partially problematic, exploitative, or self-exploitative. So maybe these two complexes are related, painting on the one hand and work seen from a sociological perspective on the other. Ok, so I'm thinking out loud right now.

JB: This thesis is a bit too dramatic for me (laughs).

MS: I was struck by a repetition in the new works, in that you again show yourself as a comic figure, like you've done in the past—as Clippy, for example, that useless assistant tool created by Microsoft. Or as a shrunken-head monster. It's obviously striking that you work with a lot of self-portraits, but why do you choose to present yourself as a buffoon?

JB: Hmm, good question. When you make yourself kind of absurd as a protagonist, I essentially find that to be a relatable approach. Not taking yourself so seriously as an author, that's maybe a reflection of my overall attitude, as I find authorship in the sense of a personal production of things to be fairly suspect in general. I'm aware that there's a huge number of influences that shape my work. And as I said before, coincidences are no problem for me, they're a key productive part of my work. And that might also reflect something of my presence as their author. Honestly, I've never thought about that, but it seems somehow plausible to me that in this ludicrous figure of the creating person (laughs) there's a lot of freedom. But as a conscious vulnerability. I certainly don't present as authoritarian. In the end, someone's work is nothing more than an assertion. That's always the thing I found coolest about art: everyone just asserts all the time and it just depends on who makes the coolest, most exaggerated, strangest, most audacious, and nevertheless most plausible assertion—and for that exact reason, authority in the classic sense doesn't count for anything. For me that was always a liberating moment in art. So I present myself as an author in all sorts of weird, ridiculous poses, so that I can question my position.

MS: But maybe also be mindful of revealing problematic implications of a liberal understanding of the artist, who serves as the inaugurator of deregulation within the world of labor. Is a kind of ridiculousness for you the only way for you to anchor yourself in something like making art, then?

JB: Let's just say I'm a participant observer in this whole circus. Making art is problematic and grotesque in so many ways, not least because of these entanglements you have to work within. My basic feeling is one of ambivalence; there are so many things that I think are meaningful and amazing about the form of existence I lead, but there are an incredible number of its aspects that I find dubious. I can't separate all these positive and negative aspects, because they somehow all belong together for me. I'm not saying this is a productive approach, it's just my honest approach. This arena isn't really one in which I can take sides. I believe, or hope, that my works take both this involvement and this moral dilemma seriously, and that they don't try to dispel them or to conduct any evasive maneuvers. And that this can lead to results that are super problematic, but simultaneously full of insight, as they don't attempt to demonstrate that which you generally already know. Instead, they formulate honest questions. In my work, there's always a fundamental doubt as to whether I can actually cast my lot with a particular side, and even about the idea of whether that very thing could be a quality. An artistic or philosophical quality, at least, I'm not speaking about a political quality or anything. There's a clear difference there for me. Art shows how the world *could* be, not how it *should* be. In my opinion, this is its really specific potential.

1342657

Eat and be eaten | 2018

zlig<<

Untitled (yummi) | 2018

BRILON REALISM
eight works for a yacht

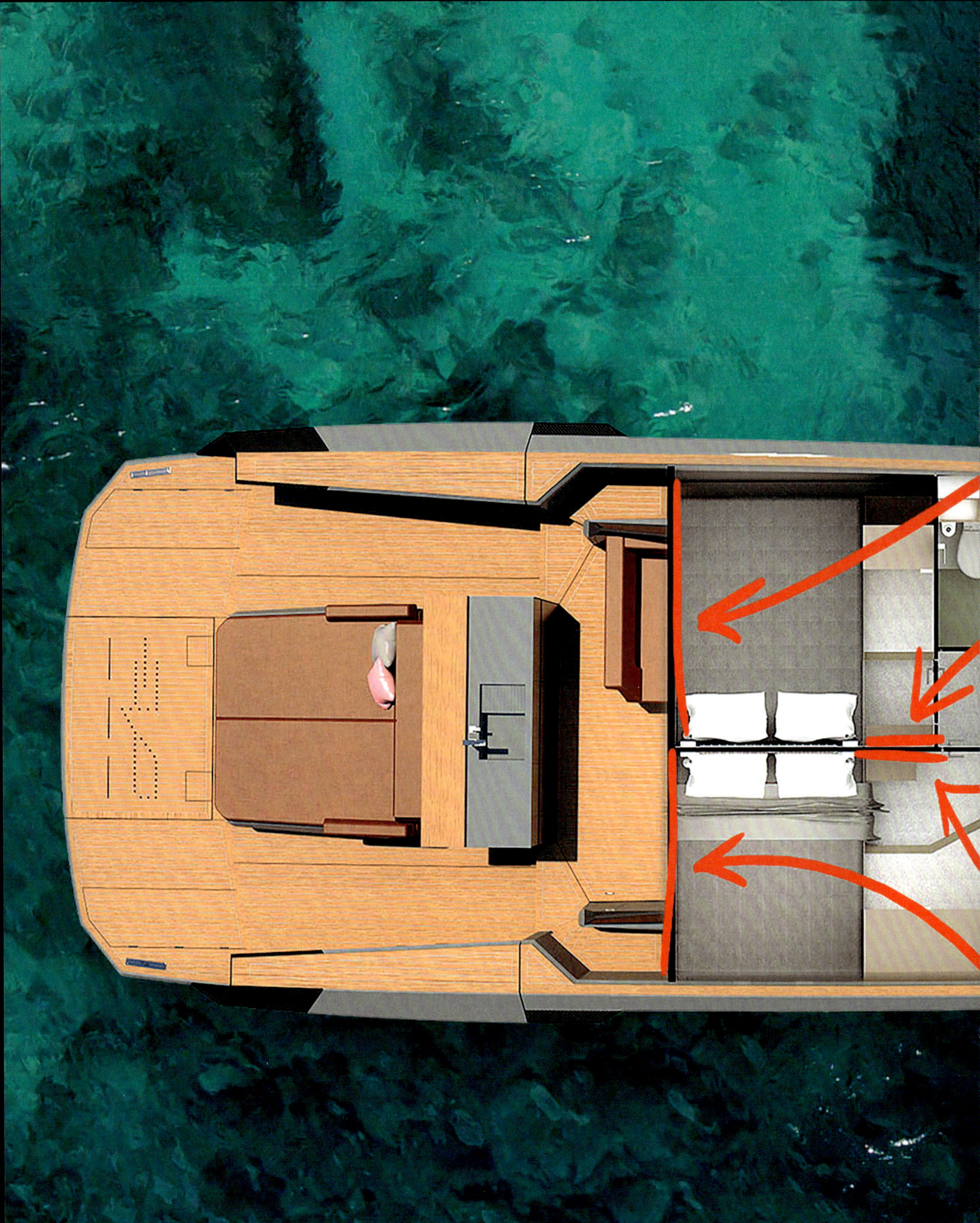

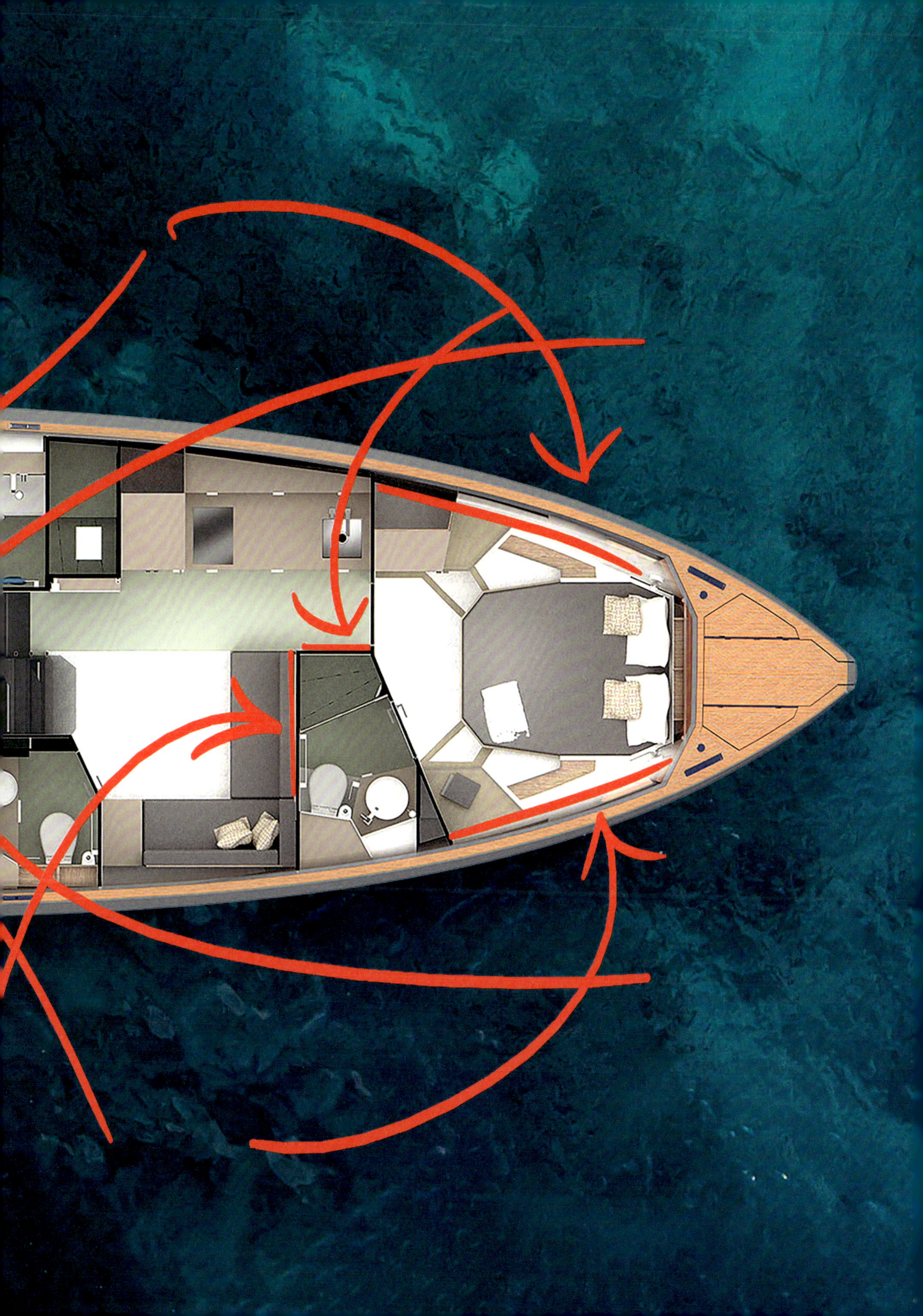

REALISM

REALISM

R
I

L

K-F203

ICEMAN
K-F203

HA$E
FUSS

Rabbit for Lui | 2018

Untitled (experiences) | 2016

penci
Soft
harder edge
paint
tradit. pencil
grainy

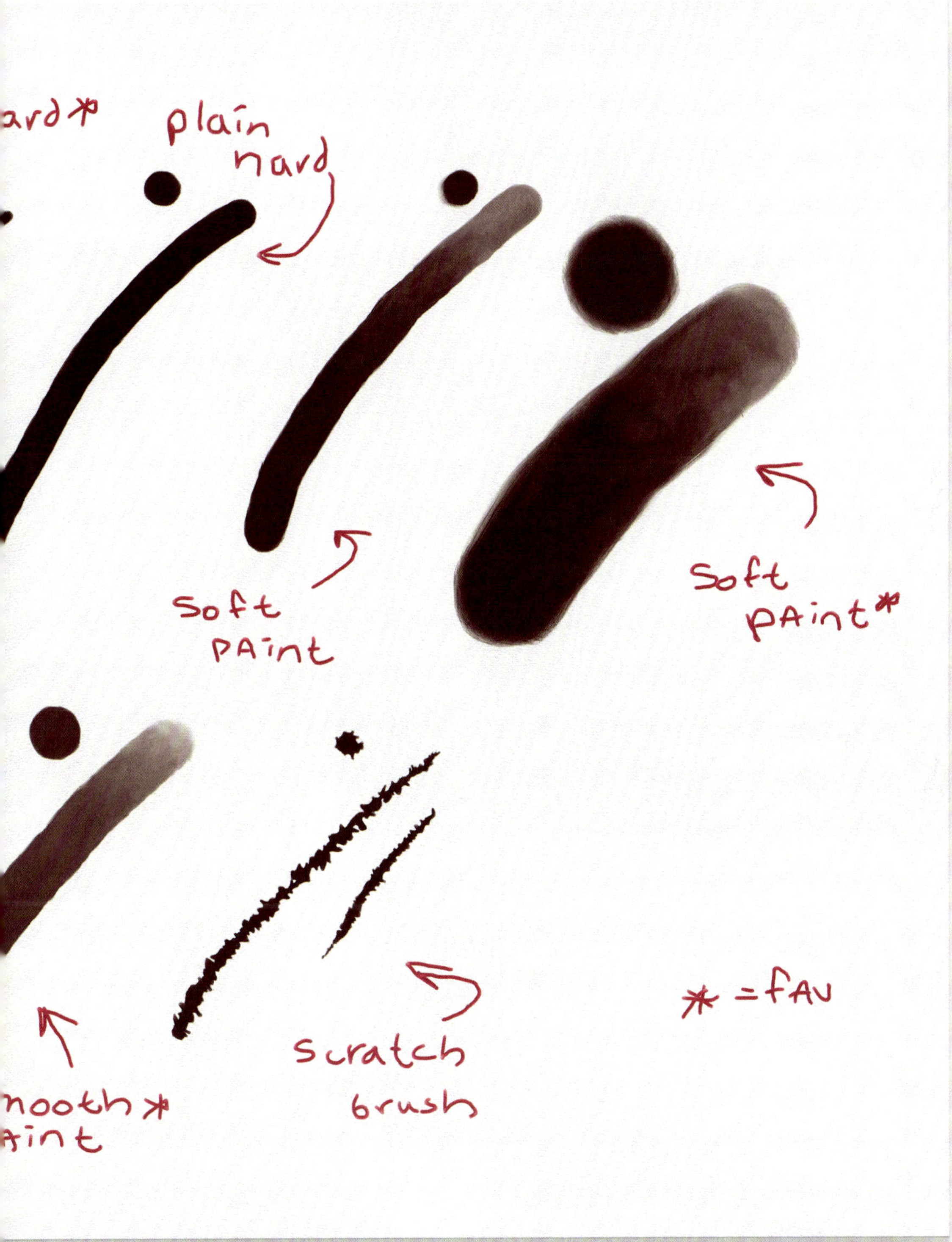
plain hard
soft paint
soft paint*
scratch brush
* = fav

Diazepam 5mg - #3 ("The Preacher") I 2017

Untitled (Desktop) I 2021

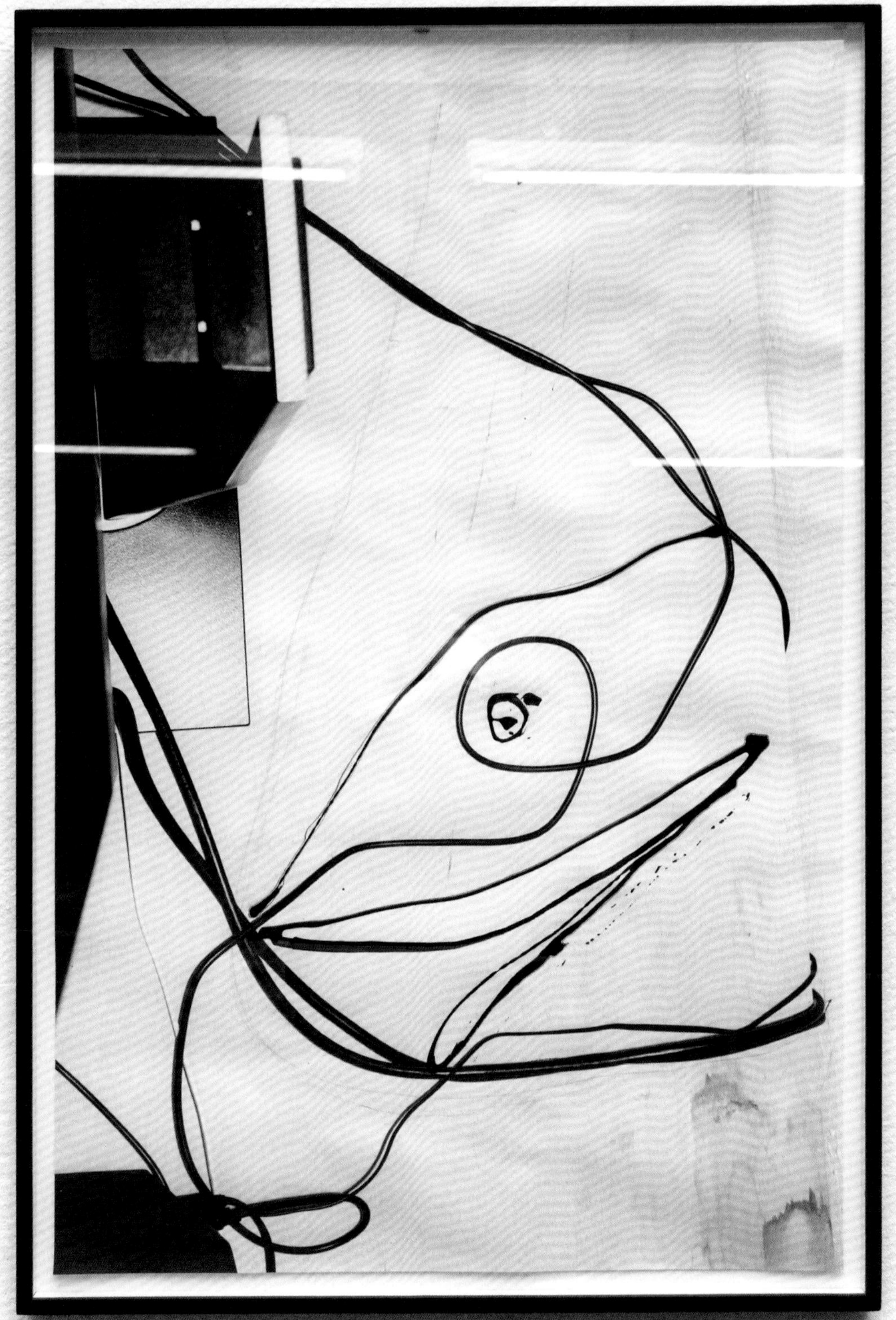

Untitled (workhorse) I 2017

Delusional Self Portrait | 2018

Quick Sundays Trip (Individual transportation bad) | 2020

Art Business As Usual

Art Business as Usual | 2015

Profit

Monday, 11:10 AM:
"I just finished a new drawing and titled it *'Think Outside the Box.'* The result's really convincing. It's definitely one of my more ambivalent and complex works. It starts at the bottom of a deep valley, soars to unimaginable heights and then tragically crashes, but with an open outcome – a shimmer of hope remains, delicately shown with only the suggestion of upward curves. This afternoon my creative team will start a four by four meter copy of it. Most of my clients won't really know how to appreciate this one. But that's hardly a problem - I earn more than enough to afford some experiments. My clients' everyday lives, mostly in the financial sector, are complicated enough. Art shouldn't be complex and unsettling for them, or open up too many questions. They're intoxicated with abstract money and mathematical models every day; abstraction in art couldn't even touch that. The reason's simple: Their world of abstractions is connected with real power and you can't really say the same for art."
Thursday, 10:55 AM:
„We installed one of my sculptures from the
session and made my way with the
The first time he saw one of the *Growth*
few) lows. He said they were simple and
I didn't have anything to add to that."
Monday 2:30 PM:
"I've just had a meeting with some representatives of the Ministry for Cultural Development from a big city not far from here. Their
than expected and are now set for significant growth. The local government recently started a branding campaign to promote the
in public spaces. They want to make the city more attractive for creative high potentials, i.e. highly qualified employees. As part of the
the new found prosperity of the region. Unfortunately their current budget isn't exactly luxurious. They tried to negotiate a hefty
included in their contemporary art museum's collection with all the corresponding positive effects on my market prices. Blablabla. I
hate doing business with governmental bureaucrats, or at least the representatives of so called western democracies. They're always
to even shake their hands. I was so pissed off about the precious time they'd stolen."

airport of one of my biggest collectors today. Usually I don't dirty my hands with that kind of work, but the guy's just too important of a customer. So I canceled my midday yoga
ralled by what he called its 'positive aura.' According to him, he was deeply moved because the sculpture seemed to be a symbol of his career until now with all its highs and (very
clarity yet contradictory, like life itself.
d by the recent financial crisis, but they're recovering faster
e particularly interested in installing monumental artworks
ire one of my Growth sculptures that perfectly symbolizes
at my sculpture, when purchased, would immediately be
hose old-fashioned appreciation strategies for ages. I really
ated. Of course I declined their ridiculous offer and refused
Tuesday 11:40 PM:
"Alright, enough for today. I've just gotten home. Time to change and finally get to bed.
I don't know why, but sometimes I get the feeling that I work too much. All these great ideas in my head keep me up at night. It's amazing but also a burden ... Maybe I should take a vacation to a place without any art or culture. But where can you find that these days? It seems more and more hopeless the more I think about it ..."

ple
py
are
ch

Monday 2:30 PM:

"I've just had a meeting with some representatives of the Ministry for Cultural Devel
than expected and are now set for significant growth. The local government recently
in public spaces. They want to make the city more attractive for creative high poter
the new found prosperity of the region. Unfortunately their current budget isn't e
included in their contemporary art museum's collection with all the corresponding
hate doing business with governmental bureaucrats, or at least the representatives c
to even shake their hands. I was so pissed off about the precious time they'd stolen.'

nt from a big city not far from here. Their economy was hit especially hard by the recent financial crisis, but they're recovering faster
d a branding campaign to promote the recent developments and they're particularly interested in installing monumental artworks
e. highly qualified employees. As part of the the plan they want to acquire one of my *Growth* sculptures that perfectly symbolizes
luxurious. They tried to negotiate a hefty bargain with the argument that my sculpture, when purchased, would immediately be
e effects on my market prices. Blablabla. I haven't been depended on those old-fashioned appreciation strategies for ages. I really
lled western democracies. They're always underfunded and overcomplicated. Of course I declined their ridiculous offer and refused

Tuesday, 9:55 AM:
"I had a meeting with the Chief Strategist of my department for *Expansion Strategies & New Markets* this morning to discuss the current state of affairs. I recently put together a team of local experts to aid my expansion into growing Asian markets. Their main task is to identify cultural and legal pitfalls in order to preclude artistic controversies well in advance. Though researching the interests and aesthetic preferences of the economic and political elites of the respective countries is also part of their responsibilities. The goal is ultimately to compile a catalogue of guidelines with possible themes and motifs for artworks, which would then form the basis of further work by me and my creative team.
My team already presented some of these motifs to me today that are safe in many ways, both in terms of their acceptance within our target group and also in terms of possible ethical, religious or moral controversies. In addition, it was also reported that my people have managed to come into direct contact with the Chinese Ministry of Culture, which could give the planned sale increases there a notable boost."
Wednesday 1:50 PM:
"Yesterday I traveled to the *Middle East* to discuss the final details of a project that I'm planning in collaboration with the government of a small but extremely wealthy
in a park in the capital.
You can think what you want about the politics of these countries, but our business collaboration has only proven to be comfortable so far. Money almost doesn't play a
even a critical public to question the artistic quality of my work or to stigmatize the purchase as a waste of taxpayer's money. The same goes for 'guided democracies' a
some call oppression means security to others. It isn't as easy to separate the world in good and evil as the pundits would have us believe.."
LIFE ISN'T ABOUT
FINDING YOURSELF
LIFE IS ABOUT CREATING
YOURSELF

ental sculpture to be installed
ardly bureaucratic. There isn't
uthoritarian leadership. What
Profit
ing the final stress test for one of my *Positive Development* sculptures. Again it's an outdoor sculpture and thus the procedure. The piece's buyer was worried about whether the piece's bit too unspecific, so I suggested integrating the word 'profit' in order to make the symbolism a bit less ambiguous. Of course it's too easy to laugh at his take on art. It's too cheap. It's nts don't like to go to the museum and read catalogues or books about art, but they just have more important things to do. That's why they really appreciate it when you can meet evel and take their educational background into consideration. That's exactly what my work does. It's a celebration of what my collectors know and love the most: wealth and its ement. I offer them objects that inflate their cultural capital and simultaneously distinguish them as philanthropists and friends of art. My clients don't think of the vast sums my works antage, rather they see it as a potential profit in terms of distinction. So one could reasonably speak of a real *win-win* situation."
Wednesday, 9:35 AM:
"This morning I decided to walk to work. People like me, people professionally involved in *'culture'* enjoy an occasional experience of nature all the more so. My property is situated somewhat outside the city in a pretty rural area. It's important for me to keep work and free time separated spatially. A good *work-life balance* is a high priority. For example, I try to keep strictly defined working hours, even if good intentions can't always be followed through.
In my free time, I try to stay as far away from art as I can. Nonetheless I've charged a team in my department of *Expansion Strategies & New Markets* with checking all relevant information channels daily and visiting important international exhibitions when necessary, so I can keep track of current trends and developments. Every second Monday, I take an hour to have myself briefed accordingly. That way, I don't have to personally deal with all the rubbish my competitors are constantly putting out into the world."

Friday, 3:30 PM:

"Here you're seeing the final stress test for one of my *Positive Development* sculptures. Again it's an outdoor s
message was a bit too unspecific, so I suggested integrating the word 'profit' in order to make the symbolis
not like my clients don't like to go to the museum and read catalogues or books about art, but they just h
them on their level and take their educational background into consideration. That's exactly what my wo
constant enlargement. I offer them objects that inflate their cultural capital and simultaneously distinguish t
cost as a disadvantage, rather they see it as a potential profit in terms of distinction. So one could reasonab

e and thus the procedure. The piece's buyer was worried about whether the piece's ess ambiguous. Of course it's too easy to laugh at his take on art. It's too cheap. It's re important things to do. That's why they really appreciate it when you can meet . It's a celebration of what my collectors know and love the most: wealth and its philanthropists and friends of art. My clients don't think of the vast sums my works k of a real *win-win* situation."

Wednesday, 3:05 AM:
"Last night, I had a fantastic dream, simultaneously inspiring and uplifting. After the global expansion of my business model had finally been accomplished, there seemed to be only one suitable challenge left: reaching for the stars, literally. In my dream, I'm sitting in my favorite yoga position on the surface of a planet while all these great ideas for new works circle around me followed by fantastic and useful business tools that would help me to actually execute them. There are millions of stars around me, each one of them a new market waiting to be conquered. It's terribly cold out here but that won't stop my intergalactic expansion. *'Master of the Universe'* was the last thing I thought before waking up freezing and shivering. I got up, made a few quick sketches for a new series of sculptures, took two sleeping pills and then went back to bed. Nonetheless, it still took at least an hour before I could get back to sleep."
Friday, 5:35 PM:
"Before any of my outdoor sculptures leave the studio, they have to undergo a stability test, which, if my schedule allows,
going to a market trader from London, if I remember correctly. The series was relatively well received by critics, at least com
wishes of a small capitalist elite without producing any kind of artistic surplus value, whereas these works were praised
incomprehensibility, off against the raw reality of the materials and their tremendous heaviness. They often draw parallel
literalness of their presence. Rather they're 'representations of a capitalist abstraction whose effects are exceedingly real a
Though it's not like I care about these people's opinions or that I depend on their good intentions. These days art history isn
enforce their idea of taste. I've found my place in the new art history ages ago, far away from all the professional culture
seriously."

his work from the *Business Abstractions* series is
so far. I'm usually accused of just illustrating the
bstraction of the growth represented, in all its
, but my works don't exhaust themselves in the
oundaries between abstraction and realism.'
people who, with all their money and influence,
g, as far as I'm concerned, is hardly to be taken
Thursday, 2:55 PM:
"A big art magazine recently suggested I write a comprehensive article about my artistic work. While we were talking about the choice of the relevant photos, it quickly became clear to everyone involved that photos showing the usual procedures in my studio were out of the question. We all agreed that we shouldn't give the readers such an image of the artist. As efficient and successful as my working process is, it just has too little sex *appeal*. People are into the eccentricity of the artist, the magic of the creative process and the fascinating places they manifest themselves in. Offices, people in suits, desks and potted plants are about the last thing they want to see in an art magazine; they've got enough of that in their everyday lives. In the end we agreed to leave out the studio photos and stage me as a charismatic and mysterious artist instead. A good decision in every way – the results aren't anything to sneeze at."
CONCEPT
COLOUR
FORM
SHAPE
ART
TIME
COSTS
s the perfect opportunity to explain the foundations of my artistic work to my new interns. My introduction mainly helps to preclude any eventual misunderstandings about the kind of creativity that'll
m. Most of them are art students and are usually under the naive impression that some kind of radical, free thinking is expected or some kind of ability to question the everyday in an unconventional or
Those kinds of absurdities might be justifiable in an art school but are definitely out of place in my studio. To keep a business of this scale running, you need problem solving skills that focus on concrete
o applies to my *creative department* where most of these interns end up.
with artists or other professionals in the culture industry. They're used to being poorly paid and have an extreme work ethic that usually approaches self-exploitation. The idea of getting a foot in the door
omehow bearable for them. They practically get paid in lottery tickets – difficult to imagine that model working anywhere else..."

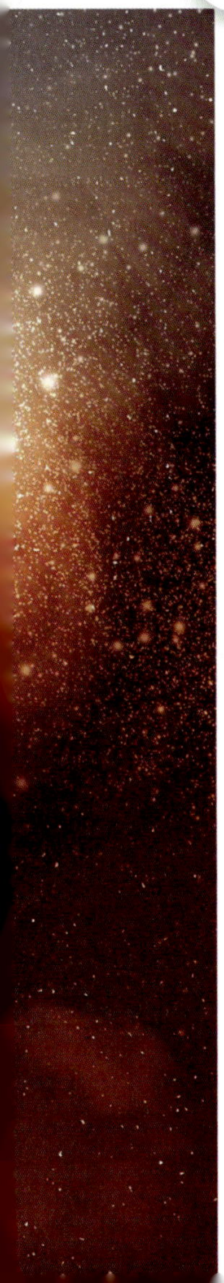

Friday, 5:35 PM:
"Before any of my outdoor sculptures leave the studio,
going to a market trader from London, if I remember cor
wishes of a small capitalist elite without producing any
incomprehensibility, off against the raw reality of the m
literalness of their presence. Rather they're 'representati
Though it's not like I care about these people's opinions
enforce their idea of taste. I've found my place in the n
seriously."

ve to undergo a stability test, which, if my schedule allows, I like to conduct myself. This work from the *Business Abstractions* series is he series was relatively well received by critics, at least compared to the others I made so far. I'm usually accused of just illustrating the f artistic surplus value, whereas these works were praised for skillfully playing the abstraction of the growth represented, in all its and their tremendous heaviness. They often draw parallels to minimal art of the 60's, but my works don't exhaust themselves in the capitalist abstraction whose effects are exceedingly real and thus question the old boundaries between abstraction and realism.'
depend on their good intentions. These days art history isn't written but *made* by the people who, with all their money and influence, history ages ago, far away from all the professional culture pessimists whose whining, as far as I'm concerned, is hardly to be taken

No More Business As Usual | Artist book | 58 Seiten | 2015

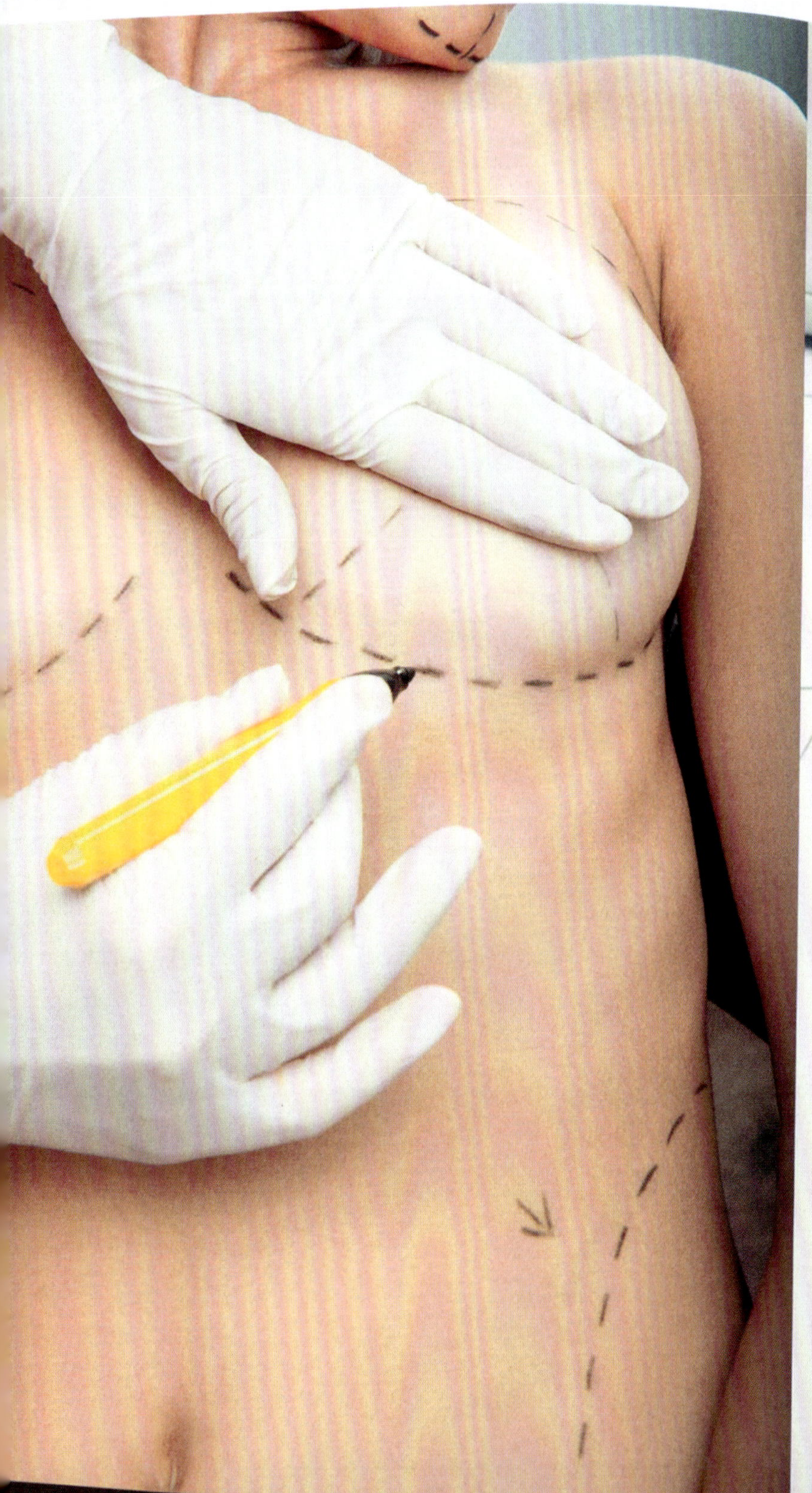

65%

5%

RE BUSI

XXL | XXX

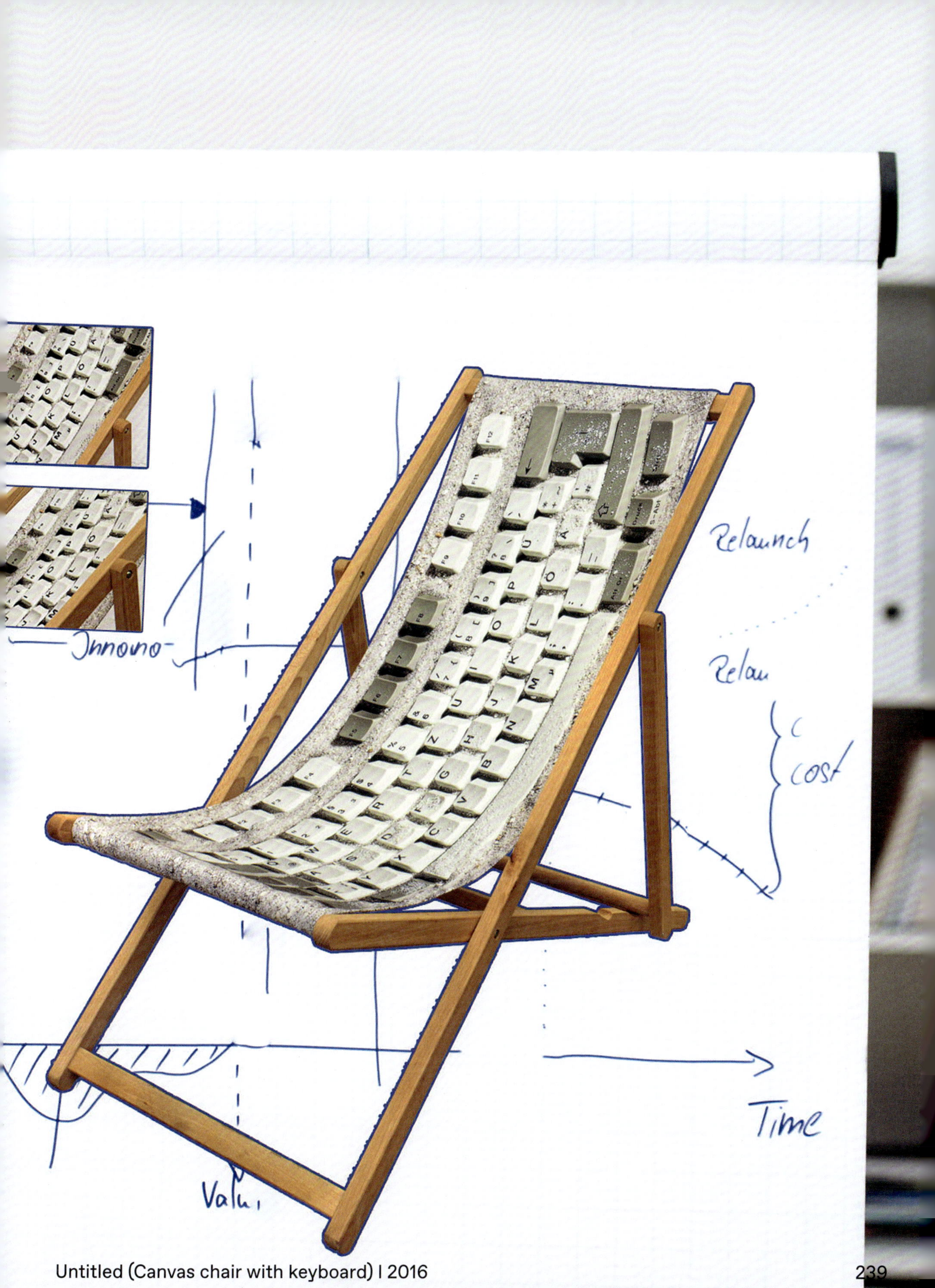

Untitled (Canvas chair with keyboard) | 2016

XXL | XXX | underpass Ebertplatz | Cologne | 2017

24/4

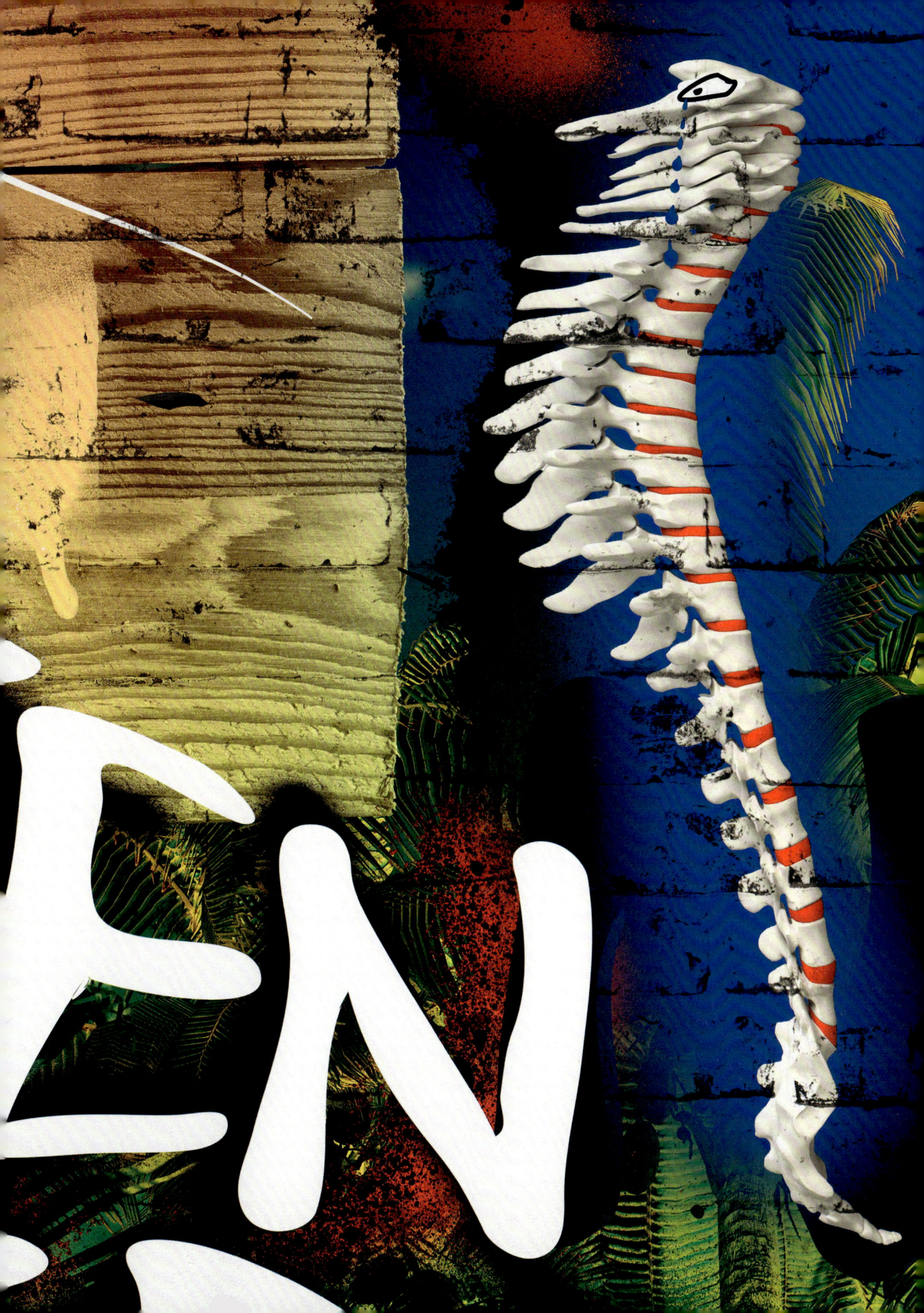

You‘re Fired

FRIEND

You‘re Fired | Brennan & Griffin Gallery | New York City | 2016

Worst Friendly Takeover Ever | 2016

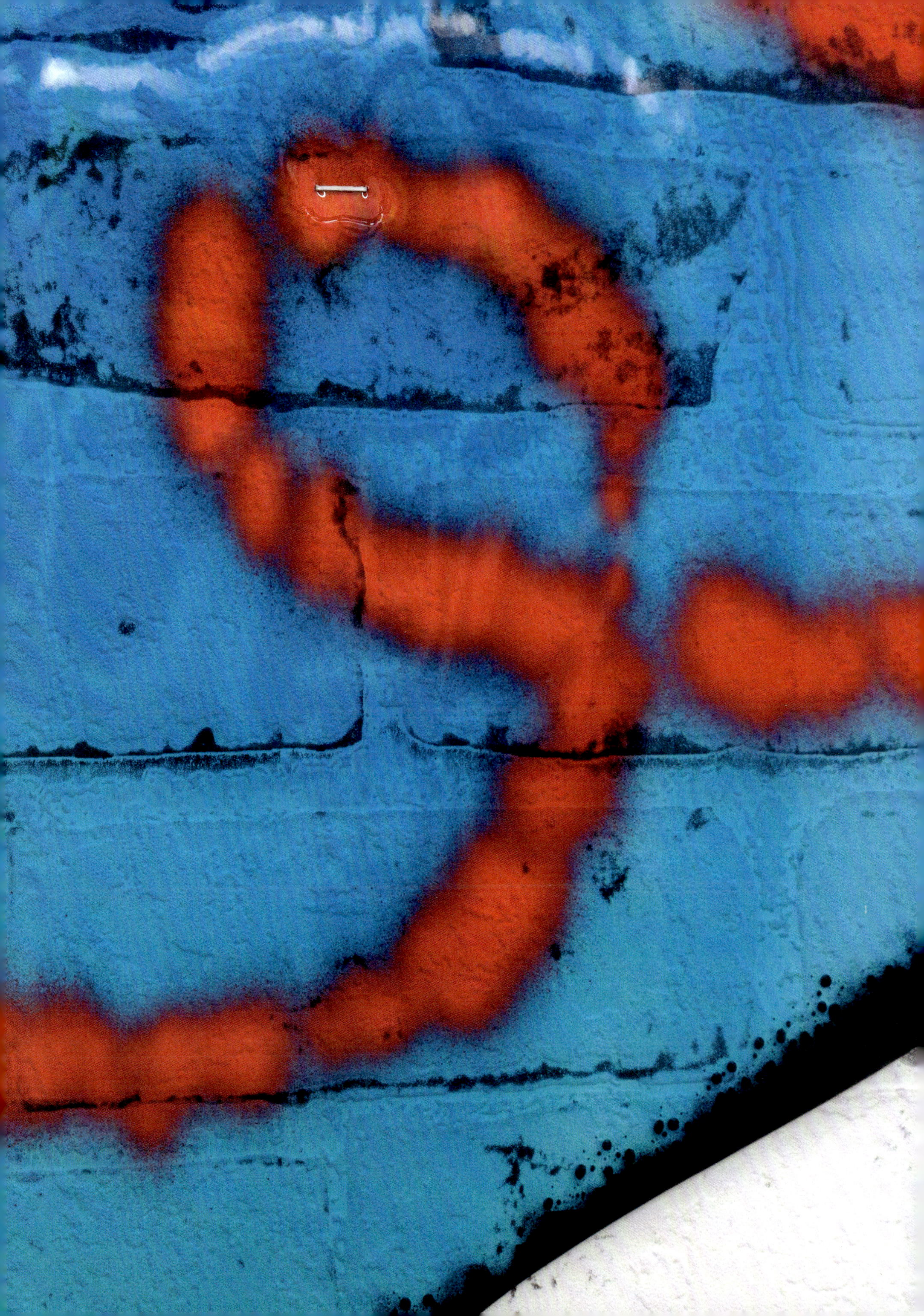

PRESSU
RE

Accident I 2016

Natural Selection | 2016

Hobby? What Hobby?!?? I 2016

WHAT

The Sky is the Limit I 2016

WORSE
TIVE DES
TRUCTI ON
EVER

Worst Creative Destruction Ever | 2016

I Love My Job

I Love My Job | Parkhaus Düsseldorf | 2015

Fuck Your Ideas (artbusinessasusual.tumblr.com) I 2015

Distinct or Extinct | 2015

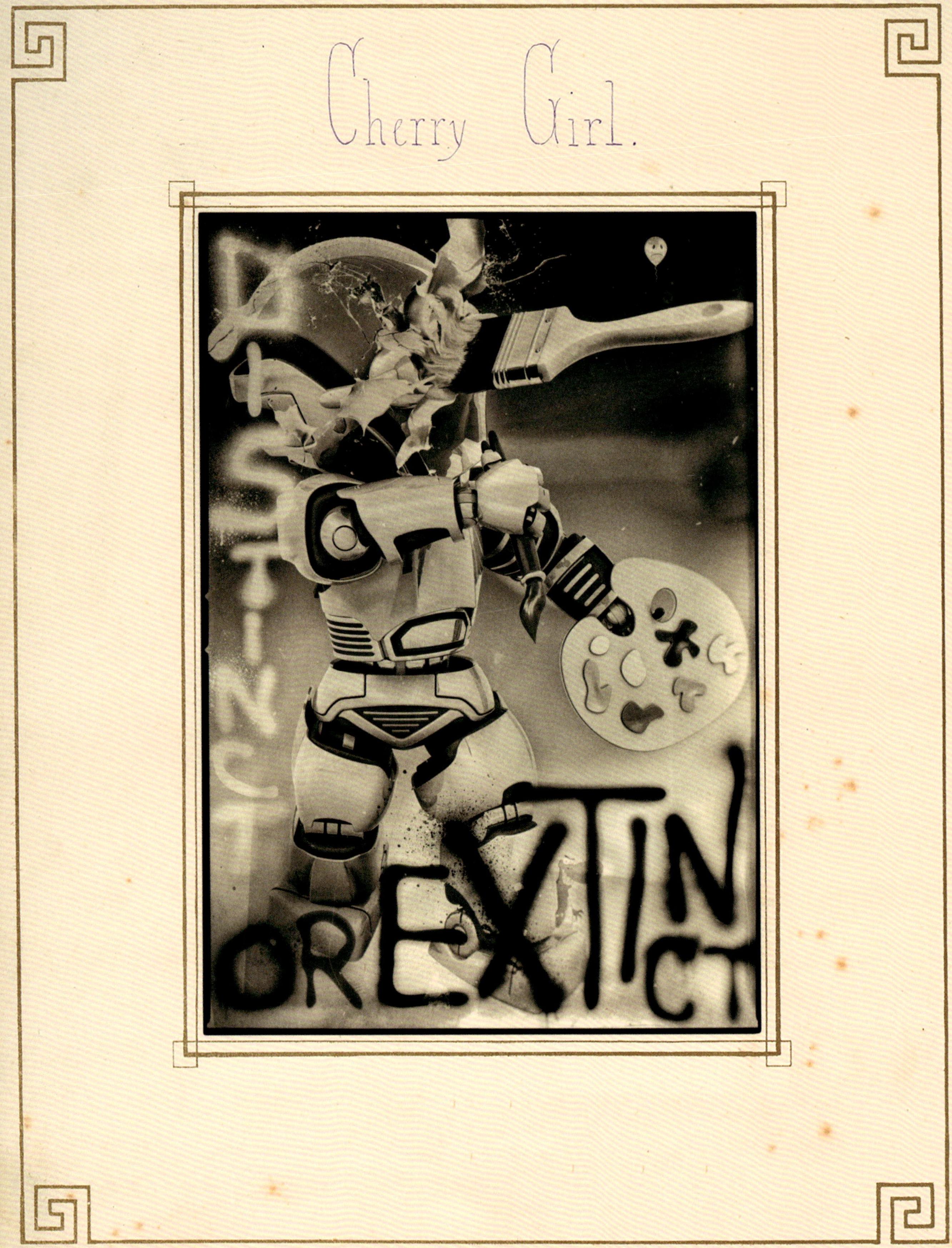

Distinct or Extinct (New old version) | 2017

Spring 2015: En Plein Air

YOUNG
BUSINESSMAN
RELAXING WHIL
PAINTIN

to be connected around the clock
afraid we'll miss something important. There
to step out and create 'quiet zones' to
technology and unwind, giving our time to
Color choices follow the same minimalistic,
taking a cue from nature rather than
or mechanically manipulated. Soft, cool
with subtle warm tones to create a soothing
the everyday hustle and bustle."
Executive Director, Pantone Color Institute®
– Pantone Fashion Color Report für die Früh-
2015

“Many feel compelled to b
because we are afraid we’ll m
is a growing movement to ste
disconnect from technology
stop and be still. Color choic
‘en plein air’ theme, taking
being reinvented or mecha
hues blend with subtle wa
escape from the everyday hu
Leatrice Eiseman, Executive D
Aus „En Plein Air“ – Pantone F
lingssaison 2015

Quote from Pantone Fashion Color Report | Window lettering

connected around the clock ss something important. There out and create 'quiet zones' to nd unwind, giving our time to follow the same minimalistic, cue from nature rather than ically manipulated. Soft, cool n tones to create a soothing le and bustle."

ector, Pantone Color Institute® shion Color Report für die Früh-

YOUNG
BUSINESSMAN
RELAXING WHILE
PAINTING

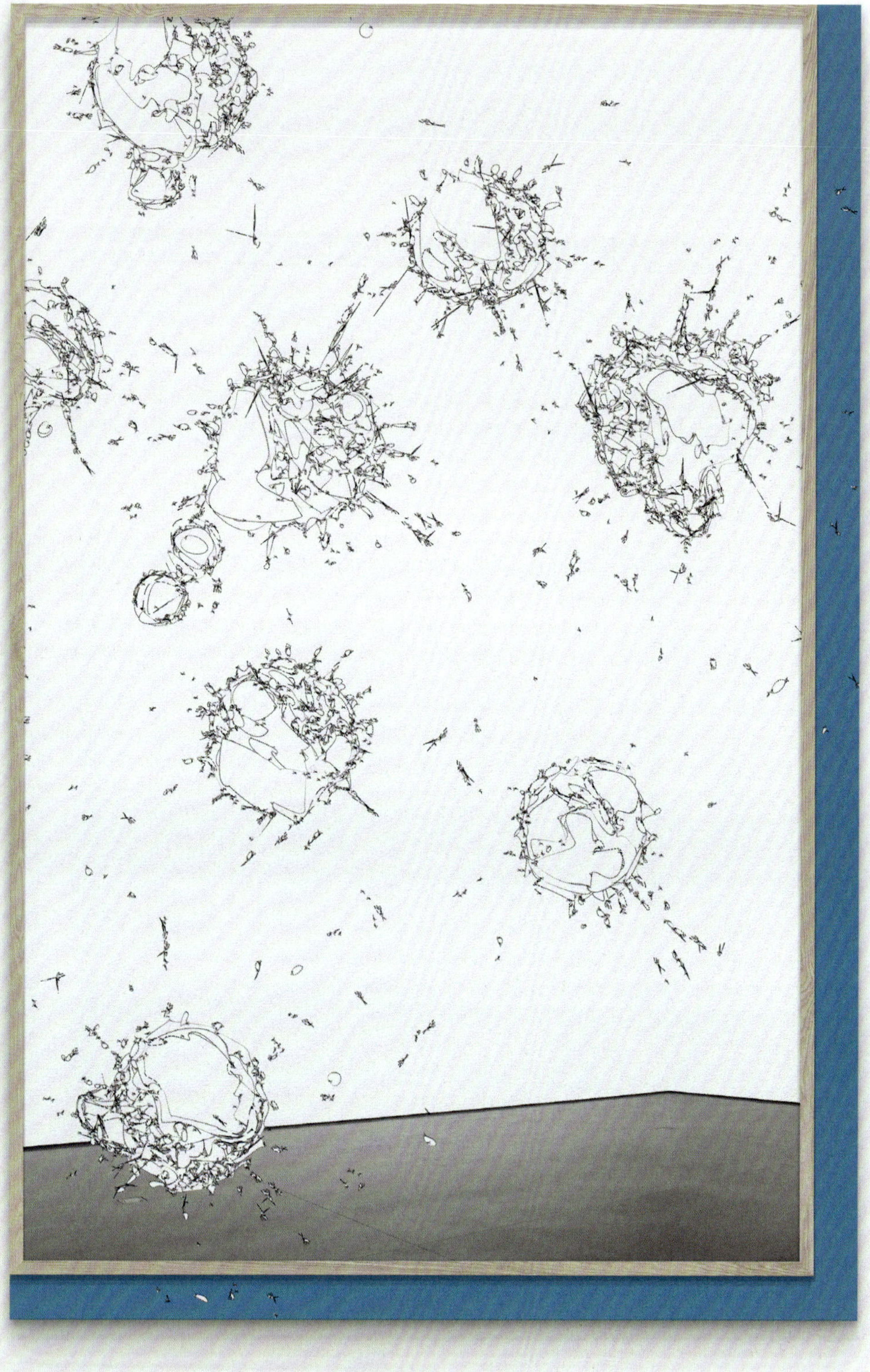

YOUNG
BUSINESSMAN
RELAXING WHILE
PAINTING

YOUNG BUSINES RELAXIN PA

SMAN
G WHILE
AINTING

BEAUTIFUL
YOUNG WOMAN
CREATING
SCULPTURE
ARTIST RELAXING
IN HIS STUDIO

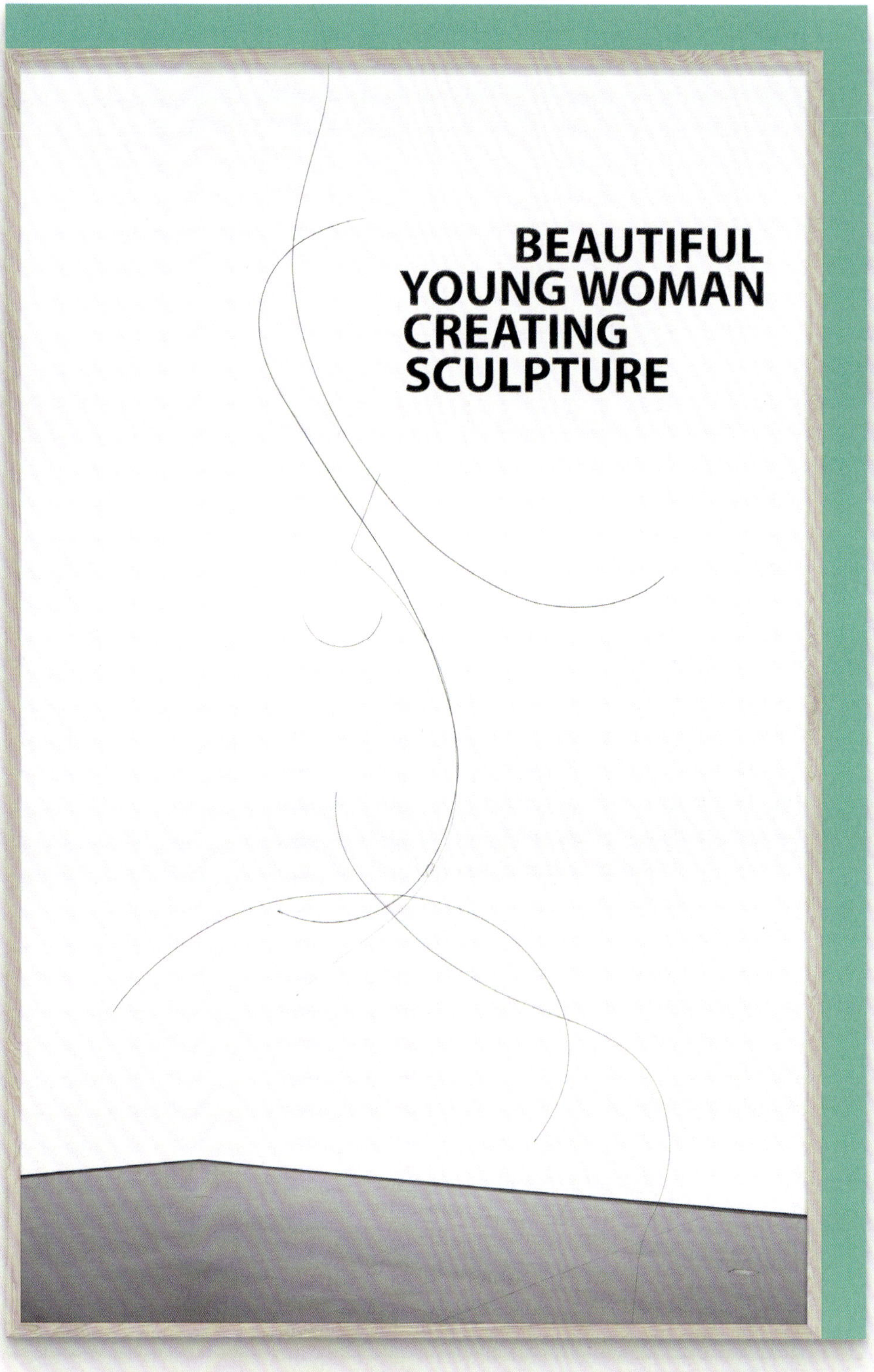
BEAUTIFUL
YOUNG WOMAN
CREATING
SCULPTURE

ARTIST RELAXING
IN HIS STUDIO

Beautiful Young Woman Making Art – Nr. 1, 2 & 3 | 2015

production / reception
Produktion / Rezeption

Produktion / Re

zeption

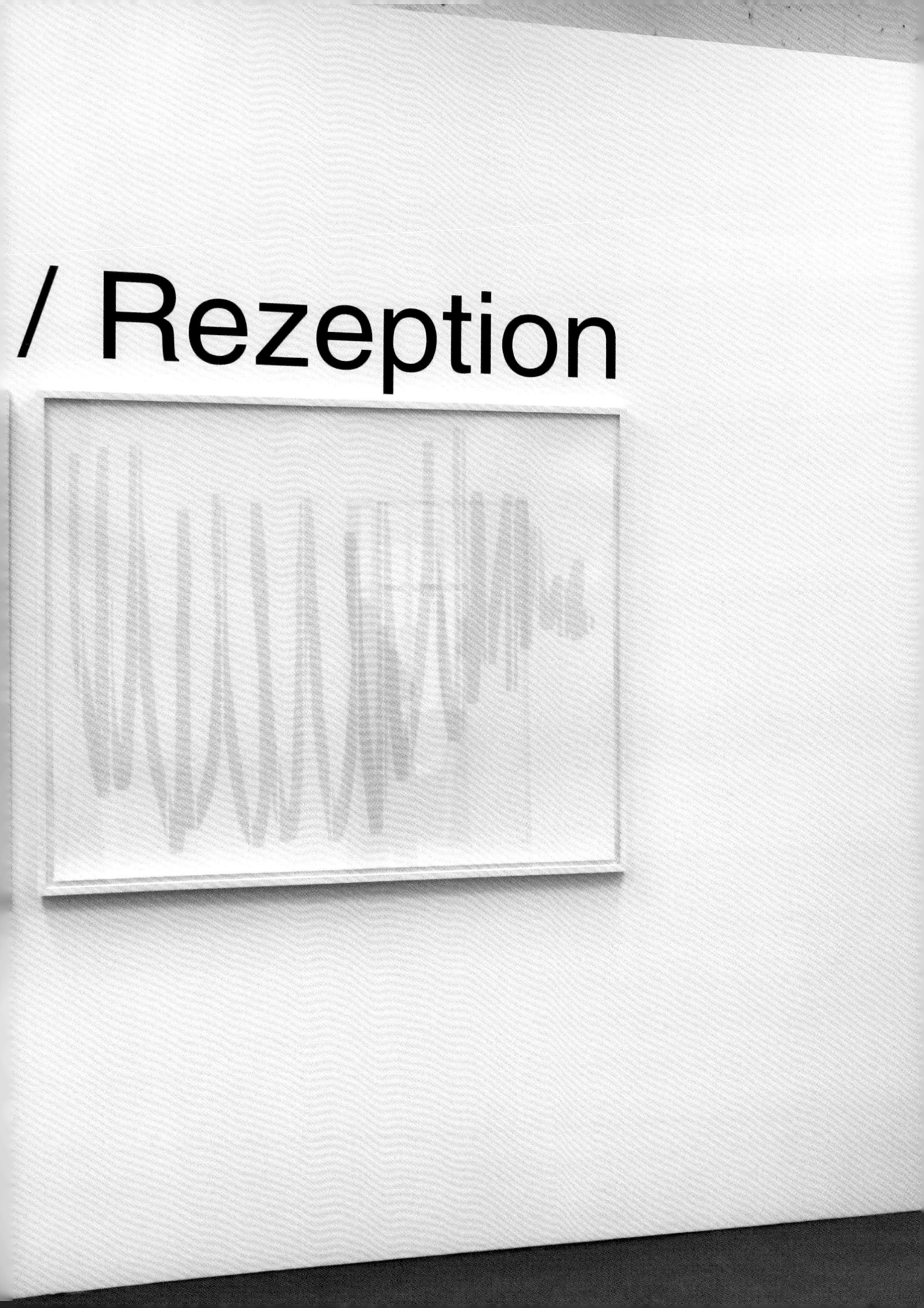
/ Rezeption

production

tute, poi
academic
lective m
synthesise
levels, pla
ality, narra
processua
ceived, the
regressive,
diversified,
mous, articu
al, holism, pi
tiation, exemp
ing, post-avant
cal, relational, h
val, differentiation
undermining, post-
multilayered, genre
al, personal viewpoint,
aze, facets, formal voca
textual meaning, quest
ething, medially constru
n the work, painterly ges
ompression, evoking, dia
the absent, suggesting,
material process, poetic,
omething, surrogate, implic
e, resonance chamber, col-
bstance, suggest, light up,
ion form, interpretive
r, irritation, materi-
ceptive processes,
y meant, re-
recourse,
nce,
gazeimn
conteire, perc
tiation,t, ironically
ing, post-avant ce, sugge
cal, relational, form, in
meaning, questiinti cal ga
medially constrmdensing,
pairoometying with
in tt somethin
bvert, sp

painting practice, recourse, regressive, inher-
ent, articulation, insistence, diversified, dis-
positive, affirmation, autonomous, articulate,
reflect, categorical, relational, holism, pictorial, a-perspectival, differentiation, exemplary,
set something in the work, painterly gesture,
tic, work immanent, the absent, suggesting,
openness, intersection, material process, poetic, constitute, point to something, surrogate
undermining, post-avantgardist, universal,
multilayered, genre boundaries, experimen-
tal, personal viewpoint, appropriation, critical
gaze, facets, formal vocabulary, condensing,
contextual meaning, questioning, playing with
something, medially constructed, set something in the work, painterly gesture, subvert,
spatial compression, evoking, dialectic, wo
immanent, the absent, suggesting, openness
intersection, material process, poetic, constitute, point to something, surrogate, implicit,
academic, genuine, resonance chamber, col-
lective memory, substance, suggest, light up,
synthesised, presentation form, interpretive
genuine, resonance chamber, colle
ory, substance, suggest, light up, sy
presentation form, interpretive leve
on, shimmer, irritation, materiality,
structure, perceptive processes, pr
ets, formal vocabulary, condensing
meaning, questioning, playing with
medially constructed, set somethin
work, painterly gesture, subvert, sp
pression, evoking, dialectic, work ir
the absent, suggesting, openness

production / rec

ption

uggerieren, aufscheır
tationsform, Bedeutuı
ıangieren, Irritation, M
:ruktur, Wahrnehmun
, dekonstruieren, iron
thesenhaft, malerische
ssiv, inhärent, Artikula
sifiziert, Dispositiv, Af-
rtikulieren, reflektie-
tiv, Affirmation, autonom
ren, kategorisch, rela-
it, piktural, aperspekti-
ung, exemplarisch, Re-
inieren, postavantgardis-
chichtig, Genregrenzen,
Sichtweise, vereinnah-
, Facetten, Formenspra-
zusammenhänge, hinter-
elen, medial konstruiert,
n, malerischer Gestus,
he Verdichtung, evozie-
immanent, das Abwe-
Offenheit, Schnittstelle,
tisch, konstituieren, auf
rogat, impliziert, akade-
anzraum, kollektives Ge-
uggerieren, aufscheinen,
ationsform, Bedeutungs-
angieren, Irritation, Ma-
ruktur, Wahrnehmungs-
dekonstruieren, ironisch
thesenhaft, malerische
ssiv, inhärent, Artikula-
sifiziert, Dispositiv, Af-
rtikulieren, reflektie-
iv, Affirmation, autonom,
ren, kategorisch, rela-
it, piktural, aperspekti-
ung, exempl arisch, Re-
inieren, post vantgardis-
chichtig, Ge egrenzen,
Sichtweise, ereinnah-
Facetten, F menspra-
usammenh e, hinter-
elen, mediε nstruiert,
, malerisc Gestus,
he Verdich vozie-
immanent, bwe-
ffenheit, S telle,
isch, kon: , auf
rogat, imp kade-
anzraur s Ge-
ıggerier inen,
ationsfo ungs-
angier Ma-
ruktur, gs-
dekon isch
hese e
ssiv, i -
sifiz

\
r
ł
kc
im
ra
ger
tati
cha
Stru
raur
gerie
tation
chang
exean
exrimer
ren, ka
piktura
exempla
postavar
Genregr
weise, ver
ten, Form
menhäng
medial kon
malerische
Verdichtung,
manent, das
heit, Schnitt
konstituieren,
impliziert, akademisch, genuin, Reson
raum, kollektives Gedächtnis, Substan
gerieren, aufscheinen, synthetisiert, P
tationsform, Bedeutungsebenen, bes
changieren, Irritation, Materialität, na
Struktur, Wahrnehmungsprozesse, p
rarnehmurves Gedäclektıtnis, Sdäc
raurn, irorcheinen, synthnthetisiert
pikturaнschıdeutungsebeвbenen, b
postavaadistisch, universsenalin, e
Gennplari, experimentell, uniniere

penen, bespielen,
erialität, narrative
rozesse, pro
emisch, genug-
s Gedächtnz, sug-
ıeinen, synererren-
aufschelonsfo, syntig,
enzieruenzieruht-
erminierrminieret-
al, Ganzheitlichkeit,
Ausdifferenzierung,
ation, unterminieren,
versell, vielschichtig,
ıtell, eigene Sicht-
tischer Blick, Facet-
rdichten, Sinnzusam-
ı, mit etwas spielen,
as ins Werk setzen,
ergraben, räumliche
dialektisch, werkim-
e, suggerieren, Offen-
rialprozess, poetisch
s verweisen, Surrogat
, genuin, Resonanz-
chtnis, Substanz, sug-
synthetisiert, Präsen-
gsebenen, bespielen,
Materialität, narrative
ungsprozesse, pro
ktives Gedäonz, sug-
ıfscheineısiert, Präser
, Bethnnn, bespielen
sentation, untermiotive
universell, vielschicht
nzeiintell, eipene Sich
ational, Ganzheitlichk
visch, Ausdifferenzieru
äsentation, unterminie
n, universell, vielschich
erimentell, eigene Sich
en, kritischer Blick, Fa
e, verdichten, Sinnzus
ragen, mit etwas spiel
t, etwas ins Werk setze
us, untergraben, räuml
ieren, dialektisch, wer
wesende, suggerieren, (
e, Materialprozess, poe
uf etwas verweisen, Sur

demisch, genuin, Resoı
es Gedächtnis, Substaı
ıeinen, synthetisiert, F
deutungsebenen, bespi
tation, Materialität, narı
ehmungsprozesse, pro
n, ironisch gebrochen
, malerische Praxis, Rel
nt, Artikulation, insistie
, Rekurs, regressiv, in
ieren, diversifiziert, Di
ıtonom, artikulieren, ref
ı, relational, Ganzheitlic
visch, Ausdifferenzieri
äsentation, untermini
h, universell, vielschich
erimentell, eigene Sicht
ı, kritischer Blick, Fac
, verdichten, Sinnzusaı
gen, mit etwas spielen,
etwas ins Werk setzen,
ıntergraben, räumliche
ı, dialektisch, werkim-
de, suggerieren, Offen-
terialprozess, poetisch,
s verweisen, Surrogat,
genuin, Resonanz-
chtnis, Substanz, sug-
synthetisiert, Präsen-
sebenen, bespielen,
aterialität, narrative
sprozesse, prozessu-
ch gebrochen, rezi-
che Praxis, Rekurs,
lation, insistieren,
regressiv, inhärent,
versifiziert, Disposi-
tikulieren, reflek-
al, Ganzheitlichkeit,
sdifferenzierung,
ı, unterminieren,
ell, vielschichtig,
eigene Sicht-
r Blick, Facet-
n, Sinnzusam-
vas spielen,
erk setzen,
n, räumliche
h, werkim-
eren, Offen-
, poetisch,
, Surrogat,
sonanz-
anz, sug-
Präsen-
pielen,
rrative
rozessu-
, rezi-
ekurs,

f
c
a
tic
vis f
pra ı,
tisc s
exp ell
men che
che, chte
frager it et
etwas s Wer
unterg ıben,
ren, dialektisc
sende, sugge
Materialproze
etwas verweis
misch, genuir
dächtnis, Sub
synthetisiert,
ebenen, bespi
terialität, narr
prozesse, pro
gebrochen, re
Praxis, Rekur
tion, insistiere

ım, kollektives Ge-
eren, aufscheinen,
sform, Bedeutungs-
eren, Irritation, Ma-
r, Wahrnehmungs-
nstruieren, ironisch
enhaft, malerische
inhärent, Artikula-
iert, Dispositiv, Af-
ulieren, reflektie-
Affirmation, autonom,
ı, kategorisch, rela-
piktural, aperspekti-
ng, exemplarisch, Re-
ieren, postavantgardis-
hichtig, Genregrenzen,
Sichtweise, vereinnah-
Facetten, Formenspra-
zusammenhänge, hinter
elen, medial konstruie
en, malerischer Gestus
che Verdichtung, evozie
kimmanent, das Abwe-
, Offenheit, Schnittstell
etisch, konstituieren, a
urrogat, impliziert, aka
onanzraum, kollektive
, suggerieren, aufsche
ntationsform, Bedeut
changieren, Irritatio
Struktur, Wahrnehm
al, dekonstruieren, i
t, thesenhaft, maleri
ressiv, inhärent, Ar
ersifiziert, Disposit
, artikulieren, refle
sitiv, Affirmation,
ieren, kategorisch
keit, piktural, ape
ierung, exemplar
minieren, postav
elschichtig, Genr
ne Sichtweise,
ck, Facetten, Fo
nzusammenhä
spielen, medial
zen, malerisch
liche Verdicht
rkimmanent
, Offenheit, S
etisch, kon
urrogat, im
onanzraur
, suggerie
ntations
changier
Struktur
al, dekc
t, these
ressiv,
ersifiz

gerieren, aufschein
tationsform, Bedeut
changieren, Irritatio
Struktur, Wahrnehm
raun, aliztives Genial
gerieren, auheinensta
exempn, mm, Beverssc
postavantgaisch, um
Genregrenzexperimsell
wesch, Retentrseien, e
ren, kategorisch, relat
piktural, aperspektivis
exemplarisch, Repräser
postavantgardistisch, ur
enregrenzen, experim
eise, vereinnahmen, k
n, Formensprache, ver
enhänge, hinterfragen,
dial konstruiert, etwa
lerischer Gestus, unter
dichtung, evozieren, dia
nent, das Abwesende, s
Schnittstelle, Materia
stituieren, auf etwas ver
iziert, akademisch, gen
-, kollektives Gedächtn
en, aufscheinen, synt
sform, Bedeutungsebe
ieren, Irritation, Materi
r, Wahrnehmungspro
nungstives Geterialite
ironisn, aivetisvas verwe
ische Irrinisch, genuir

ert, Präsen
, bespielen,
it, narrative
se, pro
emz, sug-
t, Prsen ung,
iziert inieren,
ielschichtig,
elrie Sicht-
tech, Facet-
zheitlichkeit,
erenzierung,
nterminieren,
, vielschichtig,
igene Sicht-
r Blick, Facet-
, Sinnzusam-
was spielen,
Verk setzen,
en, räumliche
sch, werkim-
erieren, Offen-
ess, poetisch,
sen, Surrogat,
Resonanz-
ubstanz, sug-
siert, Präsen-
n, bespielen,
tät, narrative
sse, pro
litachtnug-
sen, Surrogat,
Resonanz-

ntgardiı, vi- ann m inorrnessiv, rung,
enzel, eigent-sesdifferenzierische Rig,
omahler Bltell, ei, unntell, eierecet-
egorisch, relational, Ganzheitlichkeit,
aperspektivisch, Ausdifferenzierung,
isch, Repräsentation, unterminieren,
gardistisch, universell, vielschichtig,
nzen, experimentell, eigene Sicht-
innahmen, kritischer Blick, Facet-
nsprache, verdichten, Sinnzusam-
, hinterfragen, mit etwas spielen,
struiert, etwas ins Werk setzen,
Gestus, untergraben, räumliche
, evozieren, dialektisch, werkim-
Abwesende, suggerieren, Offen-
telle, Materialprozess, poetisch,
, auf etwas verweisen, Surrogat,
ademisch, genuin, Resonanz-
ves Gedächtnis, Substanz, sug-
cheinen, synthetisiert, Präsen-
edeutungsebenen, bespielen,
tation, Materialität, narrative
ehmungsprozesse, pro
n, amplizienz, suonz, sug-
f etwas vereveisen, syen ung,
misch, genuin, Reche iniere
hizierurh, univeterminiere
antiinxperimenteielschichti

kons
impli
raum
gerie
tatio
chan
Strul
al, de
piert
regre
male
Artik
tiv, A
tiere
piktu
exem
posta
Genr
weis
ten
me
me
ma
Ver
ma
heit
kon
imp
rau
ger
tati
cha
Stru
al,
pie
reg
ma
Arti
tiv,
tie
pi
ex
pc
Ge
w
t
r
r
r

eren, auf etwas verwe ogat,
akademisch, genuin, nz-
ektives Gedächtnis, Su sug-
aufscheinen, synthetis isen-
m, Bedeutungsebener ielen,
n, Irritation, Materialitä rative
Wahrnehmungsprozess ozessu-
uieren, ironisch gebrc n, rezi-
nhaft, malerische Prax Rekurs,
härent, Artikulation, in istieren,
Praxis, Rekurs, regres v, inhärent,
insistieren, diversifiziert, Disposi-
on, autonom, artikulieren, reflek-
orisch, relational, Ganzheitlichkeit,
spektivisch, Ausdifferenzierung,
Repräsentation, unterminieren,
listisch, universell, vielschichtig,
, experimentell, eigene Sicht-
ahmen, kritischer Blick, Facet-
ache, verdichten, Sinnzusam-
terfragen, mit etwas spielen,
iert, etwas ins Werk setzen,
tus, untergraben, räumliche
zieren, dialektisch, werkim-
vesende, suggerieren, Offen-
e, Materialprozess, poetisch,
etwas verweisen, Surrogat,
nisch, genuin, Resonanz-
Gedächtnis, Substanz, sug-
ien, synthetisiert, Präsen-
tungsebenen, bespielen,
on, Materialität, narrative
mungsprozesse, prozessu
ronisch gebrochen, re
alerische Praxis, Rek

misch, gen
dächtnis, S
synthetisier
ebenen, be
terialität, n
prozesse, p
gebrochen,
Praxis, Rek
tion, insisti
firmation, a
diversifizi
artikulier
tional, Ga
visch, Au
präsent
tisch, u
experir
men,
che, v
frag
etwa
unt
rer
se
M

BAD
ART

WORKING ON
BAD ART
DOES NOT
MAKE ANY
SENSE

NOBODY NEEDS TO SEE ART THAT IS NOT REALLY GOOD

FUCK
IDEAS
THAT ARE NOT
REALLY
GOOD

All Information is
Subject to Change

All Information is Subject to Change, Brennan & Griffin Gallery, New York City | 2014

Sheet Saver (Front and Backside) | 2012

Untitled (crop) | 2013

Ink cartridge (packed, leaking) | 2011

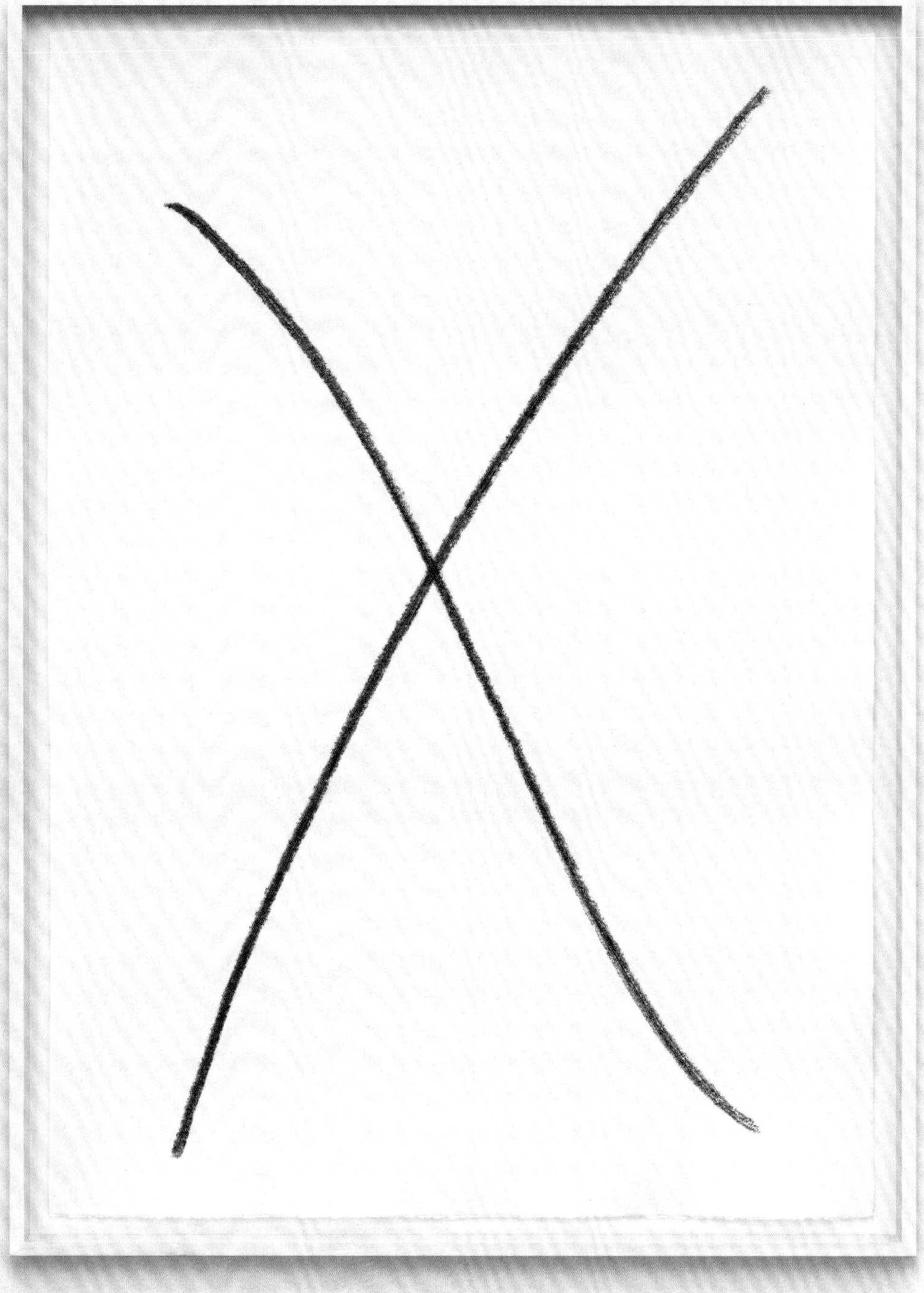

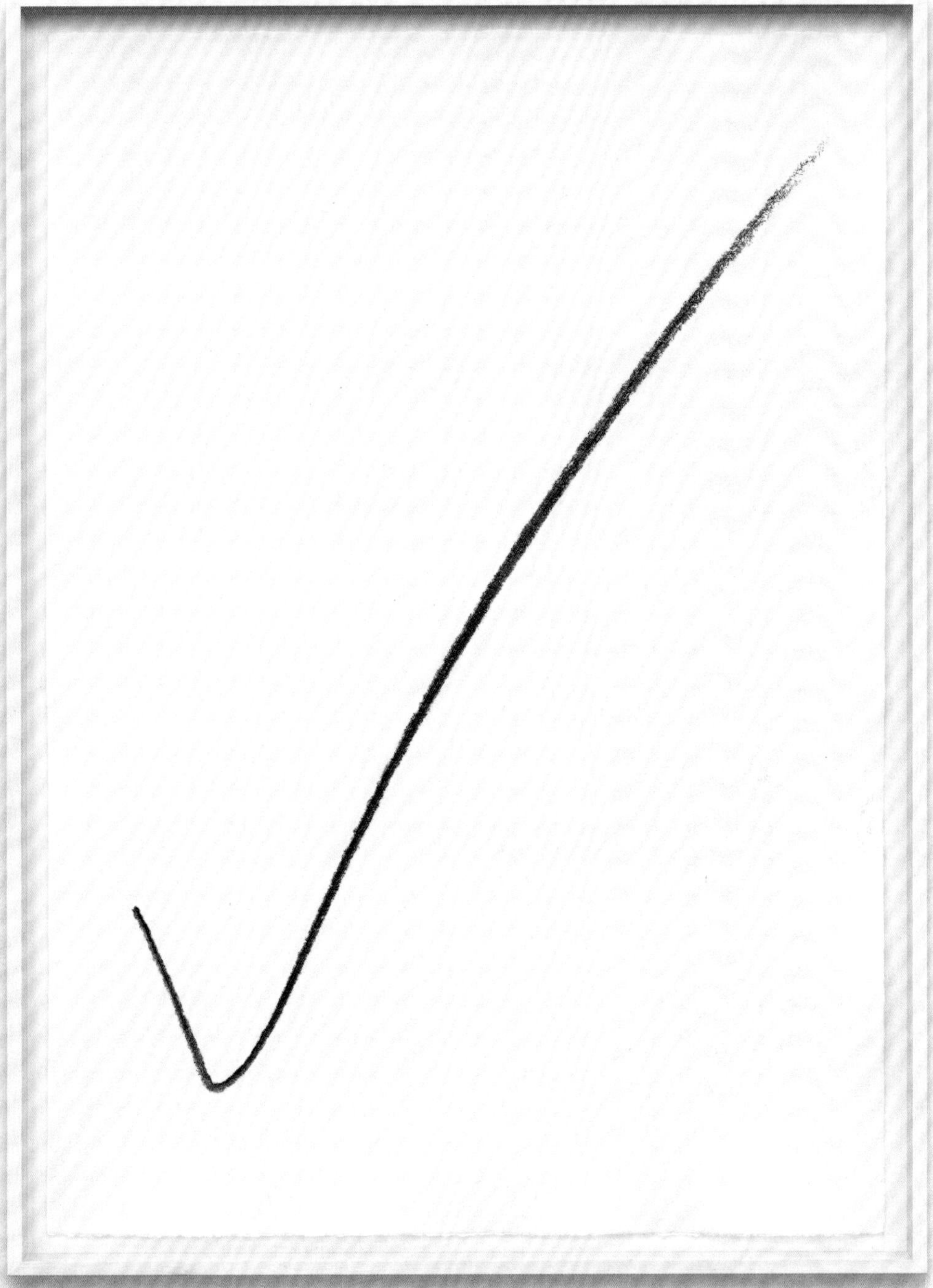

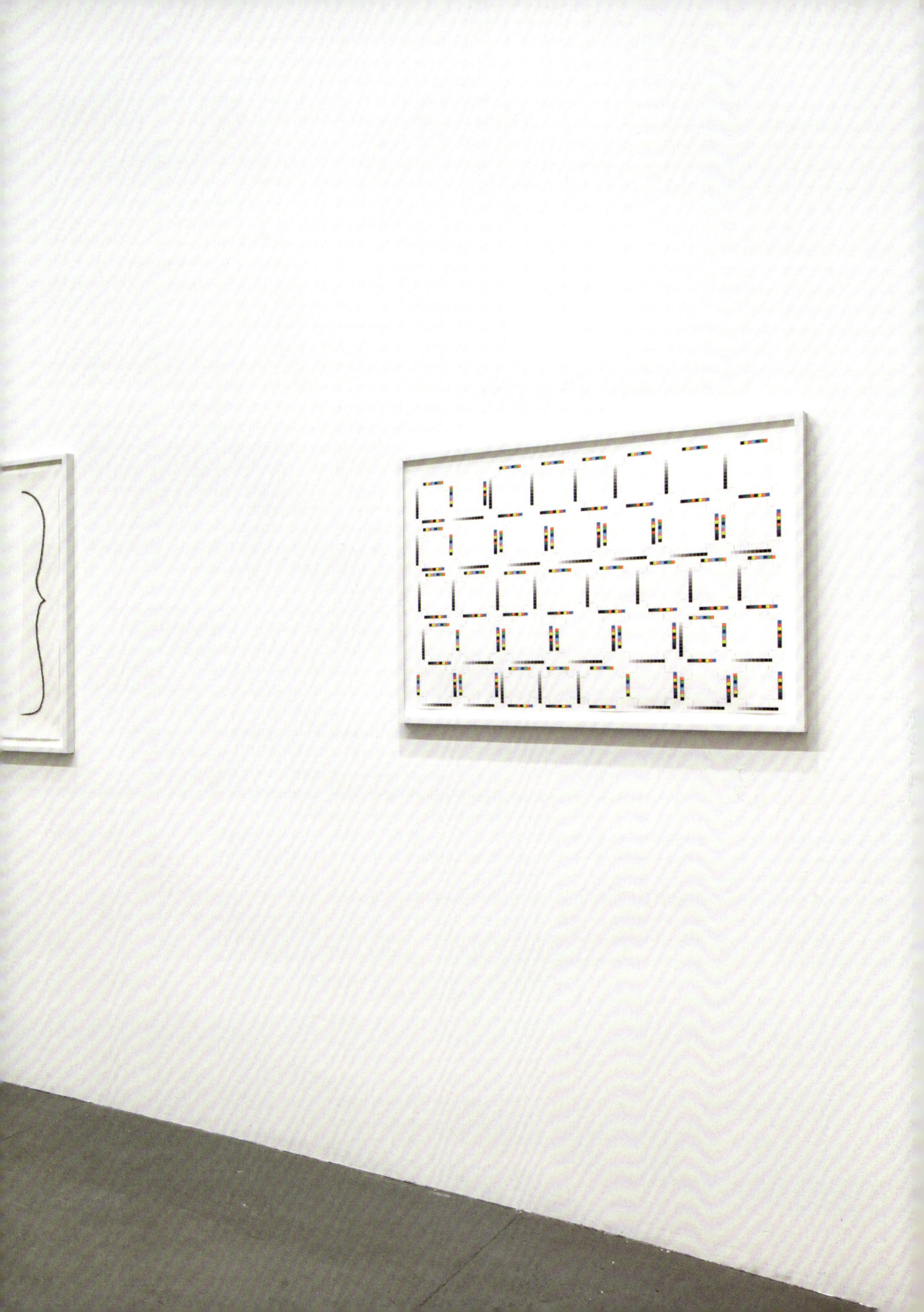

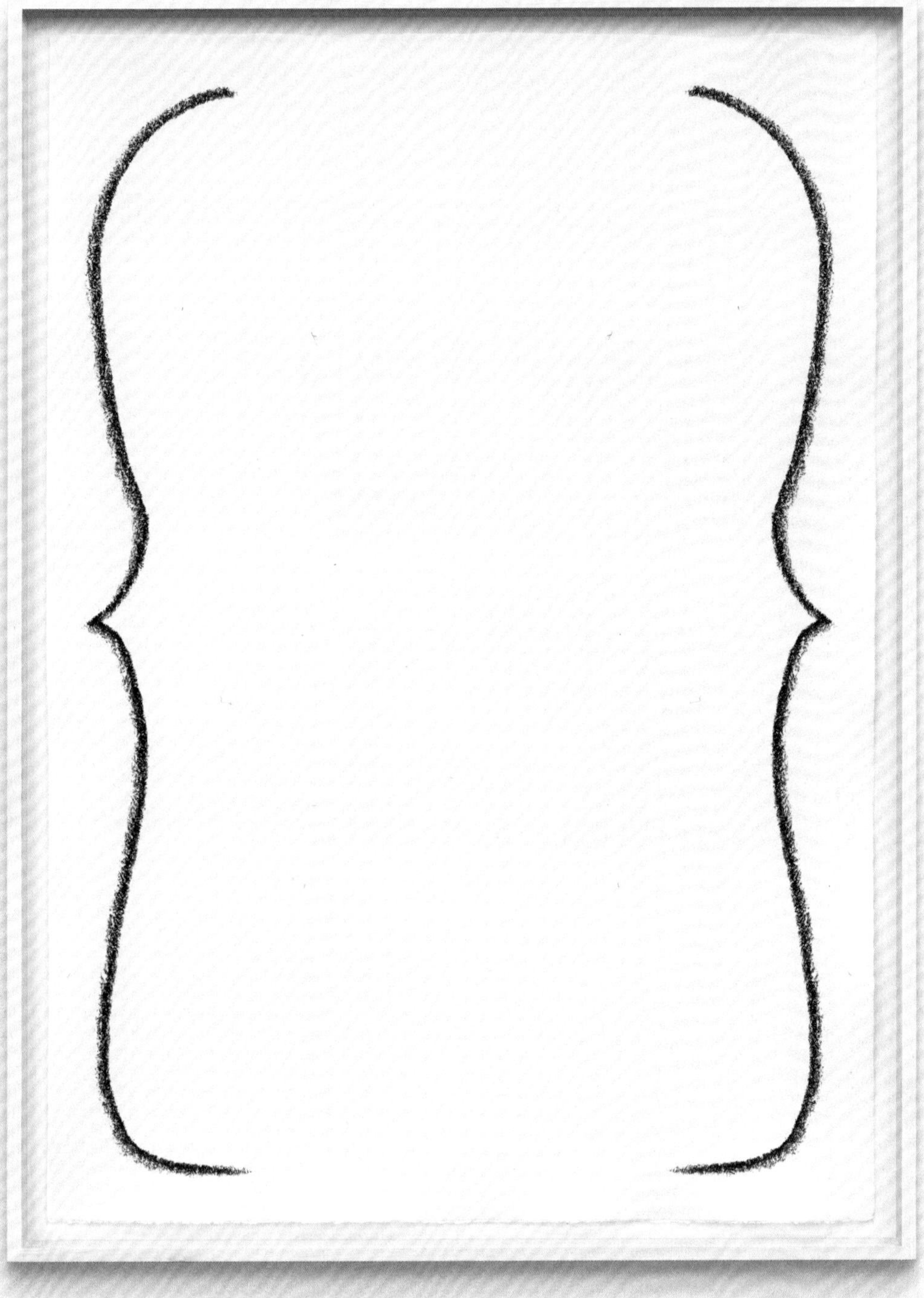

Eyebrows I 2012

Staples I 2012

Black Monochrome (40x40) | 2012

Untitled (DIN A4 sheet) | 2011

Untitled (canvas) | 2010

S. / p.

64–65 *Ohne Titel (The Show)*
Untitled (The Show),
2019
Inkjet Print auf Büttenpapier /
Inkjet print on laid paper
150 x 230 x 6,5 cm
Courtesy Galerie Petra Rinck,
Düsseldorf, Germany

66 *Der Schädling / The Pest,*
2019
Inkjet Print auf Büttenpapier /
Inkjet print on laid paper
90 x 66 x 3 cm
Courtesy Galerie Petra Rinck,
Düsseldorf, Germany

67 *The Hand That Feeds,*
2019
Inkjet Print auf Büttenpapier /
Inkjet print on laid paper
90 x 66 x 3 cm
Courtesy Galerie Petra Rinck,
Düsseldorf, Germany

68–69 Installationsansicht:
Schon Wieder Fühlen,
Petra Rinck Galerie,
Düsseldorf /
Installation view: Feeling Again,
Petra Rinck Gallery,
Düsseldorf, Germany
2019
Photo: Achim Kukulies

71 *The Jury,*
2019
Inkjet Print auf Büttenpapier /
Inkjet print on laid paper
90 x 66 x 3 cm
Courtesy Galerie Petra Rinck,
Düsseldorf, Germany

72–73 *Ohne Titel / Untitled,*
2019
Inkjet Print auf Büttenpapier /
Inkjet print on laid paper
90 x 140 x 3,5 cm
Courtesy Galerie Petra Rinck,
Düsseldorf, Germany

74 *Ohne Titel / Untitled,*
2019
Detail

#SpontexMandala
Galerie Natalia Hug,
Köln, Germany
2019

77 Werbematerial der Firma
Spontex; Vorderansicht /
Advertisement by the company
Spontex; front view

78 Werbematerial der Firma
Spontex; Rückansicht /
Advertisement by the company
Spontex; back view

S. / p.

80–81 *Spontex_007,*
2019
Detail

83 *Spontex_007,*
2019
Inkjet Print auf Büttenpapier /
Inkjet print on laid paper
140 x 90 x 3,5 cm

84–85 Installationsansicht:
#SpontexMandala,
Galerie Natalia Hug, Köln /
Installation view:
#SpontexMandala,
Natalia Hug Gallery, Cologne,
Germany
2019

86 *Spontex_008,*
2019
Inkjet Print auf Büttenpapier /
Inkjet print on laid paper
140 x 90 x 3,5 cm

87 *Spontex_005,*
2019
Inkjet Print auf Büttenpapier /
Inkjet print on laid paper
81 x 61 x 3,5 cm

88–89 Installationsansicht:
#SpontexMandala,
Galerie Natalia Hug, Köln /
Installation view:
#SpontexMandala,
Natalia Hug Gallery, Cologne,
Germany
2019

91 *Spontex_001,*
2019
Inkjet Print auf Büttenpapier /
Inkjet print on laid paper
140 x 90 x 3,5 cm

93 *Spontex_004,*
2019
Inkjet Print auf Büttenpapier,
Unterkonstruktion
aus Aluminium
Inkjet print on laid paper,
aluminum substructure
81 x 55,5 x 3,5 cm

94 *Spontex_006,*
2019
Detail

95 *Spontex_004,*
2019
Inkjet Print auf Büttenpapier /
Inkjet print on laid paper
81 x 61 x 3,5 cm

96–97 Installationsansicht:
Next Generations, Museum
Morsbroich, Leverkusen /
Installation view:
Next Generations,
Museum Morsbroich,
Leverkusen, Germany
2019

S. / p.

99 *#SpontexMandala*
(Listen to your Heart),
2018
Inkjet Print auf Büttenpapier,
gerahmt / Inkjet print on laid
paper, framed
41,6 x 31,6

100 *#SpontexMandala_HEART_001,*
2018
Detail

101 *#SpontexMandala_HEART_001,*
2018
Inkjet Print auf Büttenpapier /
Inkjet print on laid paper
140 x 90 x 3,5 cm

103 *#SpontexMandala_SMILE_001,*
2018
Inkjet Print auf Büttenpapier /
Inkjet print on laid paper
140 x 90 x 3,5 cm

105 *#SpontexMandala_HEART_001,*
2018
Inkjet Print auf Büttenpapier /
Inkjet print on laid paper
140 x 90 x 3,5 cm

106–107 *#SpontexMandala_HEART_001,*
2018
Detail

108 *Spontex_002*
2018
Inkjet Print auf Büttenpapier,
Unterkonstruktion aus
Aluminium / Inkjet print on laid
paper, aluminum substructure
81 x 55,5 x 3,5 cm

109 *Spontex_003*
2018
Inkjet Print auf Büttenpapier,
Unterkonstruktion aus
Aluminium / Inkjet print on laid
paper, aluminum substructure
81 x 55,5 x 3,5 cm

111 Installationsansicht:
Next Generations, Museum
Morsbroich, Leverkusen /
Installation view:
Next Generations,
Museum Morsbroich,
Leverkusen, Germany
2019

130-131 Interlude mit Kartoffeln und
digitaler Malerei / Interlude with
potatoes and digital painting

Interlude mit magischen Händen
Interlude with magical hands

134–135 Installationsansicht:
72. Internationale Bergische
Kunstausstellung,
Kunstmuseum Solingen /
Installation view: ↗

72. Internationale Bergische Kunstausstellung, Kunstmuseum Solingen, Germany

137 *Fressen und gefressen werden / Eat and be eaten,* 2018
Inkjet print auf transparenter Folie, Acrylfarbe, Holz, Tackernadeln, Dibond / Inkjet print on transparent foile, acrylic paint, wood, staples, Dibond
230 x 140 x 10 cm

138–139 *Fressen und gefressen werden / Eat and be eaten,* 2018
Detail

141 *nuetzlig: die Honigbiene / youseful: the honeybee,* 2018
Inkjet print auf transparenter Folie, Acrylfarbe, Holz, Tackernadeln, Dibond / Inkjet print on transparent foile, acrylic paint, wood, staples, Dibond
230 x 140 x 10 cm

142–143 *nuetzlig: die Honigbiene / youseful: the honeybee,* 2018
Detail

145 *Ohne Titel (Yummi) / Untitled (Yummi),* 2018
Inkjet print auf transparenter Folie, Acrylfarbe, Holz, Rakel, Tackernadeln, Dibond / Inkjet print on transparent foile, acrylic paint, wood, scraper, staples, Dibond
230 x 140 x 10 cm

146–147 Detail Ohne Titel (Yummi) / Untitled (Yummi), 2018

BRILON REALISM
(Eight works for a yacht)
Palma de Mallorca, Spain
2020

150–151 Lageplan / Floorplan
Außenansicht der Yacht, für deren Innenräume acht spezifische Arbeiten entworfen wurden / External view of the yacht whose interiour has been equipped with eight specifically designed artworks
2020
Photo: Studio Borlenghi

152–153 Installationsansicht: Hauptschlafzimmer / Installation view: Main bedroom
Photo: Studio Borlenghi

154–155 *Ohne Titel / Untitled,* 2020
UV Druck auf Wandpanel, versiegelt mit Plexiglas / UV Print on wall panel, sealed with Plexi glass
63 x 235 cm and 63 x 230 cm
Photo: Studio Borlenghi

156–157 Detail (S. / p. 154–155)

158–159 *Ohne Titel / Untitled,* 2020
UV Druck auf Wandpanel, versiegelt mit Plexiglas / UV Print on wall panel, sealed with Plexi glass
63 x 230 cm
Photo: Studio Borlenghi

160–161 Detail (S. / p. 158–159)

162–163 Außenansicht Yacht / Exteriour view of the yacht
Photo: Studio Borlenghi

164–165 Installationsansicht: Küche / Installation view: Kitchen
Photo: Studio Borlenghi

166–167 *Ohne Titel / Untitled,* 2020
Detail
UV Druck auf Wandpanel, versiegelt mit Plexiglas / UV Print on wall panel, sealed with Plexi glass
95 x 156 cm

168–169 *Ohne Titel / Untitled,* 2020
Detail
UV Druck auf Wandpanel, versiegelt mit Plexiglas / UV Print on wall panel, sealed with Plexi glass
95 x 70 cm

170–171 Installationsansicht: Küche / Installation view: Kitchen
Photo: Studio Borlenghi

172–173 Installationsansicht: Schlafzimmer 1 / Installation view: Bedroom 1
Photo: Studio Borlenghi

174–175 Installationsansicht: Schlafzimmer 1 / Installation view: Bedroom 1
Links: UV Druck auf Wandpanel, versiegelt mit Plexiglas / Left: UV Print on wall panel, sealed with Plexi glass
90 x 61 cm
Rechts: UV Druck auf ↗ Wandpanel, versiegelt mit Plexiglas / Links: UV Print on wall panel, sealed with Plexi glass
90 x 207 cm
Photo: Studio Borlenghi

176–177 Detail (S. / p. 172–173)

178–179 Detail (S. / p. 174–175)

180–181 Außenansicht Yacht / Exteriour view of the yacht
Photo: Studio Borlenghi

182–183 Installationsansicht: Schlafzimmer 2 / Installation view: Bedroom 2
Photo: Studio Borlenghi

184–185 Detail (S. / p. 182–183)

186–187 Installationsansicht: Schlafzimmer 2 / Installation view: Bedroom 2
Links: UV Druck auf Wandpanel, versiegelt mit Plexiglas / Left: UV Print on wall panel, sealed with Plexi glass
90 x 190 cm
Rechts: UV Druck auf Wand panel, versiegelt mit Plexiglas / Right: UV Print on wall panel, sealed with Plexi glass
90 x 66 cm
Photo: Studio Borlenghi

188–189 Detail (S. / p. 186–187)

190–191 Außenansicht Yacht / Exteriour view of the yacht
Photo: Studio Borlenghi

Interlude: Board
(moody)

194 Installationsansicht: *Hase für Lui /* Installation view: *Rabbit for Lui,* 2018

195 *Hase für Lui / Rabbit for Lui,* 2018
Inkjet print auf Büttenpapier, gerahmt / Inkjet print on laid paper, framed
33 x 33 cm

196 - 197 *Ohne Titel (experiences) / Untitled (experiences),* 2016
Links: Bedruckte Liegestühle / Left: printed canvas chairs
jeweils / each 160 x 50 x 4 cm
Rechts: Inkjet Print auf Leinwand, Holzrahmen / Right: Inkjet print on canvas, wooden frame
70 x 50 cm

S. / p.

198 – 199 *fav,*
2016
Inkjet print auf Büttenpapier /
Inkjet print on laid paper
104 x 170 x 3,5 cm

201 *Diazepam 5mg - #3*
("The Preacher"),
2017
Inkjet Print, aufgezogen
auf Holz; Bleistift, Acryl,
Tackernadeln, Schnitzerei
und Collage / Inkjet print on
laid paper, mounted on wood;
pencil, acrylic, staples;
carving and collage
47,5 x 31,5 x 2,2 cm

202 *Ohne Titel (Desktop) /*
Untitled (Desktop),
2021
Inkjet print auf Büttenpapier,
gerahmt / Inkjet print on laid
paper, framed
51,6 x 36,6
Courtesy Galerie Petra Rinck,
Düsseldorf, Germany

203 *Ohne Titel (Arbeitstier) /*
Untitled (Workhorse),
2017
Acryl und Bleistift auf
Inkjet Print, gerahmt /
Acrylic and pencil on Inkjet
print, framed
81 x 55 x 3 cm

204 – 205 *Delusional Self Portrait,*
2018
Transfer Druck: Epson Ultra
Chrome Tinte und Acrylfarbe
auf Büttenpapier; aufgezogen
auf Aluminium / Transfer print:
Epson Ultra Chrome Ink and
acrylic paint on laid paper;
mounted on aluminum
54 x 71 x 3 cm

207 *Schneller Sonntagsausflug*
(Individualverkehr böse) /
Quick Sundays Trip
(Individual transportation bad),
2020
Inkjet Print auf Büttenpapier /
Inkjet print on laid paper
98 x 60 x 3,5 cm
Courtesy Galerie Petra Rinck,
Düsseldorf, Germany

Art Business As Usual
2015/16

210 – 211 *Art Business As Usual,*
2015
Inkjet Print, aufgezogen auf
Alu Dibond; Schrauben /
Inkjet print, mounted on
Alu Dibond; screws
Jede Tafel / 90 x 190cm
each panel 90 x 190cm

S. / p.

212 – 223 *Art Business As Usual*
Einzelne Tafeln und
Detailansichten / Individual
panels and details

125 – 234 *No More Business As Usual,*
2015
Künstlerbuch / Artist book
28 x 21 cm,
58 Seiten / pages

239 *Ohne Titel*
(Liegestuhl mit Tastatur) /
Untitled
(Canvas chair with keyboard),
2016
Bedruckter Liegestuhl /
printed canvas chair
zusammengeklappt /
folded: 160 x 50 x 4 cm

XXL|XXX
Ebertplatzpassage, Köln, Germany
2017

240 – 241 Installationsansicht:
XXL|XXX,
Ebertplatzpassage, Köln /
Installation view: XXL|XXX,
underpass Ebertplatz,
Cologne, Germany
Linkes Schaufenster:
Inkjet Print auf glänzender
tranparenter Folie, Tackernadeln /
Left window: Inkjet print on
glossy transparent foile, staples
Rückwand rechtes Schaufenster:
Inkjet Print auf Papier /
Backwall right window:
Inkjet print on paper

242 – 243 Detail XXL|XXX - linkes Schau
fenster / left window

You're Fired
Brennan & Griffin Gallery,
New York City, USA
2016

246 – 247 Installationsansicht:
You're Fired,
Galerie Brennan & Griffin,
New York City, USA /
Installation view: You're Fired,
Brennan & Griffin Gallery,
New York City, USA
2016

248 – 249 *Worst Friendly Takeover Ever,*
2016
Inkjet Print auf glänzender
transparenter Folie, Struktur-
tapete, Tackernadeln /
Inkjet print on glossy
transparent foile, textured
photo wallpaper, staples
150 x 230 x 4,5 cm

S. / p.

250 – 251 *Worst Friendly Takeover Ever,*
2016
Detail

253 *Pleasure Pressure,*
2016
Inkjet Print auf glänzender
transparenter Folie, Struktur-
tapete, Tackernadeln /
Inkjet print on glossy
transparent foile, textured
photo wallpaper, staples
220 x 155 x 4,5 cm

255 *Accident,*
2016
Inkjet Print auf glänzender
transparenter Folie, Struktur-
tapete, Tackernadeln /
Inkjet print on glossy
transparent foile, textured
photo wallpaper, staples
220 x 155 x 4,5 cm

256 – 257 *Natural Selection,*
2016
Inkjet Print auf glänzender
transparenter Folie, Struktur-
tapete, Tackernadeln /
Inkjet print on glossy
transparent foile, textured
photo wallpaper, staples
150 x 230 x 4,5 cm

258 – 259 *Hobby? What Hobby?!??,*
2016
Inkjet Print auf glänzender
transparenter Folie, Struktur-
tapete, Tackernadeln /
Inkjet print on glossy
transparent foile, textured
photo wallpaper, staples
150 x 230 x 4,5 cm

260 – 261 Installationsansicht:
You're Fired,
Galerie Brennan & Griffin,
New York City, USA /
Installation view:
You're Fired,
Brennan & Griffin Gallery,
New York City, USA
2016

262 – 263 *The Sky is the Limit,*
2016
Inkjet Print auf glänzender
transparenter Folie, Struktur-
tapete, Tackernadeln /
Inkjet print on glossy
transparent foile, textured
photo wallpaper, staples
150 x 230 x 4,5 cm

264 – 265 *Worst Creative Destruction Ever,*
2016
Inkjet Print auf glänzender
transparenter Folie, Struktur-
tapete, Tackernadeln /
Inkjet print on glossy
transparent foile, textured
photo wallpaper, staples
220 x 155 x 4,5 cm

Rezeption – production / reception, Blanket Cologne Gallery / Cologne, Germany
2013

302 – 303 Links / Left:
Ohne Titel (Produktion / Rezeption)
Rechts / Right:
Ohne Titel (Produktion / Rezeption)
2013
Inkjet Prints auf Büttenpapier, gerahmt / Inkjet prints on laid paper, framed - jeweils / each
115 x 140 cm
Oben: Klebebuchstaben / Top: Vinyl lettering
Installationsansicht:
Produktion / Rezeption – production / reception, Galerie Blanket Cologne, Köln / Installation view: Produktion / Rezeption – production / reception, Blanket Cologne Gallery / Cologne, Germany
2013

304 – 305 *Untitled (production / reception),*
2013
Detail

306 – 307 Links / Left:
Untitled (production / reception)
Rechts / Right:
Untitled (production / reception)
Drawing
Inkjet Prints auf Büttenpapier, gerahmt / Inkjet prints on laid paper, framed
jeweils / each 115 x 140 cm
2013
Oben: Klebebuchstaben / Top: Vinyl lettering
Installationsansicht:
Produktion / Rezeption – production / reception,
Galerie Blanket Cologne, Köln / Installation view:
Produktion / Rezeption – production / reception, Blanket Cologne Gallery / Cologne, Germany
2013

308-309 Detail Ohne Titel (Produktion / Rezeption)
Zeichnung
2013

310 – 313 Anmerkungen zur Kunst / Notes on Art
2013

<u>All Information is Subject to Change</u>
Brennan & Griffin Gallery, New York City, USA
2014

316 – 317 Installationsansicht / Installation view: All Information is Subject to Change, Brennan & Griffin Gallery, New York City, USA
2014

318 – 319 *Klarsichthülle (Vorder- und Rückseite) / Sheet Saver (front and backside),*
2012
Inkjet Prints auf Büttenpapier, gerahmt / Inkjet prints on laid paper, framed
Jeweils / each 81 x 60 cm

320 – 321 *Ohne Titel (crop) / Untitled (crop),*
2013
Inkjet Print auf Büttenpapier, gerahmt / Inkjet print on laid paper, framed
60 x 81 cm

323 *Tintenpatrone (Verpackt, ausgelaufen) / Ink cartridge (packed, leaking),*
2011
Inkjet Print auf Büttenpapier, gerahmt / Inkjet print on laid paper, framed
81 x 60 cm

324 – 325 Links / left: *Not OK,*
2012
Rechts / right: *OK,*
2012
Inkjet Prints auf Büttenpapier, gerahmt / Inkjet prints on laid paper, framed
Jeweils / each 81 x 60 cm

326 – 327 Installationsansicht / Installation view:
All Information is Subject to Change,
Brennan & Griffin Gallery, New York City, USA
2014

329 *Klammern / Brackets,*
2012
Inkjet Print auf Büttenpapier, gerahmt / Inkjet print on laid paper, framed
81 x 60 cm

330 *Augenbrauen / Eyebrows,*
2012
Detail

331 *Augenbrauen / Eyebrows,*
2012
Inkjet Print auf Büttenpapier, gerahmt / Inkjet print on laid paper, framed
81 x 60 cm

333 *Tackernadeln / Staples,*
2012
Inkjet Print auf Büttenpapier, gerahmt / Inkjet print on laid paper, framed
81 x 60 cm

334 *Schwarzes Monochrom (40 x 40cm) / Black Monochrome (40 x 40cm),*
2012
Detail

335 *Schwarzes Monochrom (40 x 40cm) / Black Monochrome (40 x 40cm),*
2012
Inkjet Print auf Büttenpapier, gerahmt / Inkjet print on laid paper, framed
81 x 60 cm

337 Ohne Titel (DIN A4 Blatt) / Untitled (DIN A4 sheet),
2011
Inkjet Print auf Büttenpapier, gerahmt / Inkjet print on laid paper, framed
81 x 60 cm

338 – 339 Ohne Titel (Leinwand) / Untitled (canvas), 2010
Inkjet Print auf Leinwand, Nägel / Inkjet print on canvas, nails
66 x 100 cm

Konzept & Gestaltung:
Cornelius Altmann
Johannes Bendzulla

Texte:
Dr. Lilian Haberer
Moritz Scheper

Übersetzung:
Good & Cheap Art Translators, Berlin

Lektorat:
Maren Mittentzwey und Ben Caton

Bildbearbeitung:
Johannes Bendzulla

Vielen Dank an Galerie Petra Rinck, Düsseldorf.

Gesamtherstellung:
Druckerei Kettler, Bönen

Erschienen im Verlag Kettler,
Dortmund, 2022

verlag-kettler.de

ISBN: 978-3-86206-936-1

johannesbendzulla.net

Mit freundlicher Unterstützung von:

STIFTUNG KUNSTFONDS

Kunststiftung NRW

NEU START KULTUR